New Daylight

Edited by **Sally Welch**

May–August 2019

The Bible Reading Fellowship
15 The Chambers, Vineyard
Abingdon OX14 3FE
brf.org.uk

The Bible Reading Fellowship (BRF) is a Registered Charity (233280)

ISBN 978 0 85746 770 6
All rights reserved

This edition © The Bible Reading Fellowship 2019
Cover image and illustration on page 143 © Thinkstock

Distributed in Australia by:
MediaCom Education Inc, PO Box 610, Unley, SA 5061
Tel: 1 800 811 311 | admin@mediacom.org.au

Distributed in New Zealand by:
Scripture Union Wholesale, PO Box 760, Wellington
Tel: 04 385 0421 | suwholesale@clear.net.nz

Acknowledgements

Scripture quotations marked NRSV are taken from The New Revised Standard Version
of the Bible, Anglicised Edition, copyright © 1989, 1995 by the Division of Christian
Education of the National Council of the Churches of Christ in the USA. Used by
permission. All rights reserved.

Scripture quotations marked NIV are taken from The Holy Bible, New International
Version, Anglicised edition, copyright © 1979, 1984, 2011 by Biblica. Used by
permission of Hodder & Stoughton Publishers, an Hachette UK company. All rights
reserved. 'NIV' is a registered trademark of Biblica. UK trademark number 1448790.

Scripture quotations marked GNT are taken from the Good News Translation in
Today's English Version – Second Edition Copyright © 1992 by American Bible Society.
Used by permission.

Collect for Trinity 17 (p. 88) and Collect for Purity (p. 89) are copyright © 2002
Archbishops Council. Used by permission.

Canticle from Northumbria Community's Midday Prayer (p. 93) is published by Collins
in *Celtic Daily Prayer*. Adapted from Psalm 90:12, 14, 17 by Jim Patterson. Used by
permission.

A catalogue record for this book is available from the British Library

Printed by Gutenberg Press, Tarxien, Malta

Suggestions for using *New Daylight*

Find a regular time and place, if possible, where you can read and pray undisturbed. Before you begin, take time to be still and perhaps use the BRF Prayer on page 6. Then read the Bible passage slowly (try reading it aloud if you find it over-familiar), followed by the comment. You can also use *New Daylight* for group study and discussion, if you prefer.

The prayer or point for reflection can be a starting point for your own meditation and prayer. Many people like to keep a journal to record their thoughts about a Bible passage and items for prayer. In *New Daylight* we also note the Sundays and some special festivals from the church calendar, to keep in step with the Christian year.

New Daylight and the Bible

New Daylight contributors use a range of Bible versions, and you will find a list of the versions used opposite. You are welcome to use your own preferred version alongside the passage printed in the notes. This can be particularly helpful if the Bible text has been abridged.

New Daylight affirms that the whole of the Bible is God's revelation to us, and we should read, reflect on and learn from every part of both Old and New Testaments. Usually the printed comment presents a straightforward 'thought for the day', but sometimes it may also raise questions rather than simply providing answers, as we wrestle with some of the more difficult passages of scripture.

New Daylight is also available in a deluxe edition (larger format). Visit your local Christian bookshop or BRF's online shop **brfonline.org.uk**. To obtain a cassette version for the visually impaired, contact Torch Trust for the Blind, Torch House, Torch Way, Northampton Road, Market Harborough LE16 9HL; +44 (0)1858 438260; **info@torchtrust.org**. For a Braille edition, contact St John's Guild, Sovereign House, 12–14 Warwick Street, Coventry CV5 6ET; +44 (0)24 7671 4241; **info@stjohnsguild.org**.

Comment on *New Daylight*

To send feedback, please email **enquiries@brf.org.uk**, phone **+44 (0)1865 319700** or write to the address shown opposite.

Writers in this issue

Amanda Bloor is Priest in Charge of Holy Trinity Bembridge, Assistant Director of Ordinands for the Diocese of Portsmouth, and has chaplaincy responsibilities with the Army Cadet Force, the RNLI and local sailing clubs.

Amy Boucher Pye is a writer and speaker who runs the *Woman Alive* book club. She is the author of the award-winning *Finding Myself in Britain* (Authentic, 2015) and *The Living Cross* (BRF, 2016). **amyboucherpye.com**

Paul Gravelle is an Anglican priest in Auckland, New Zealand. He is a poet, writer and retreat leader and has ministered in military, urban and rural settings, supporting himself as an industrial journalist.

Tony Horsfall is a retreat leader and author based in Yorkshire. He is actively involved in his local church and tries to keep active by playing walking football and spending time with his grandchildren.

Lakshmi Jeffreys is the rector of a parish just outside Northampton. She combines this with being a wife, mother, friend, dog-walker, school governor and various other roles.

Barbara Mosse is a retired Anglican priest with experience in various chaplaincies and theological education. A freelance lecturer and retreat-giver, she is the author of *Welcoming the Way of the Cross* (BRF, 2013).

John Ryeland is ordained in the Church of England and has been the Director of The Christian Healing Mission for the past 20 years. As well as writing a number of books, including *Encountering the God Who Heals* (MD Publishing, 2017), he also writes at **healingmission.wordpress.com**.

Harry Smart is an Anglican priest and has been a mental and general hospital chaplain for many years. He has an interest in mindfulness and in labyrinths and has used them for patient and staff support.

John Twisleton is a priest, writer and broadcaster based in Haywards Heath. He is author of *Meet Jesus* (BRF, 2011), *Using the Jesus Prayer* (BRF, 2014) and *Experiencing Christ's Love* (BRF, 2017).

Penelope Wilcock writes Christian fiction, pastoral theology and Bible studies. Her books include *Spiritual Care of Dying and Bereaved People* (BRF, 2013). She blogs at **kindredofthequietway.blogspot.co.uk**.

Sally Welch writes…

One of my tasks as editor of *New Daylight* is to read through the entire issue just before I send it to BRF for further editing and proofreading. Usually I end up with my head reeling with hundreds of new ideas, reflections and insights, and it takes me a few days to return to 'normal'. This issue is no exception – for the next few months you will experience a wide range of writers, subjects and approaches, some of which will challenge, some comfort and others entertain you. All, I hope, will inform your spiritual life.

Amy Boucher Pye bravely tackles Judges, a difficult and challenging book, which seems concerned mostly with recording the many ways in which God's people turn away from him and towards other gods. However, Amy finds pockets of hope in the stories of Deborah and Gideon, and useful lessons for us all in the way that God never loses faith in his people, even when they lose faith in him. She demonstrates the way in which the Old Testament can provide depth and new dimensions to our understanding of God and of the redemption of his promises in the person of Christ.

Penelope Wilcock's reflections challenge us in a different way. Through her examination of the roles of women in the New Testament, she helps us to see that our task is to assist with the 'restoration of equality' for men and women, away from attitudes of 'dominance and subjugation', which have their roots, she asserts, as far back as the fall. She declares, however, that our challenge is to ensure that such restoration takes place 'quietly, gently, gracefully and with propriety, as befits the Christian way'.

Finally, Paul Gravelle's reflections on harvest are particularly interesting, since they come to us from the other side of the world – New Zealand. Harvest is both a universal theme and a highly place-specific phenomenon, and Paul helps us to explore both physical and spiritual harvest times.

All the reflections in this issue are written by enthusiastic and thoughtful people, whose heart for the gospel is such that they share it in the best way they can, to everyone possible. I wish you good reading!

Sally Ann Welch

The BRF Prayer

Almighty God,
you have taught us that your word is a lamp for our feet
and a light for our path. Help us, and all who prayerfully
read your word, to deepen our fellowship with you
and with each other through your love.
And in so doing, may we come to know you more fully,
love you more truly and follow more faithfully
in the steps of your son Jesus Christ, who lives and reigns
with you and the Holy Spirit, one God forevermore.
Amen

Jesus' wisdom in Luke

Even before Luke introduces us to Jesus, we can sense that his gospel is going to offer an intimate portrait of the Saviour. It is Luke who tells us about Mary's relative, Elizabeth, and her miraculous pregnancy with the child who will become John the Baptist; it is Luke who describes the sending of the angel Gabriel to Mary and her agreement to bear the Son of God. Alone among the gospel writers, Luke details Christ's birth in Bethlehem and includes a story of the boy Jesus, vividly portraying his desire to be in the temple, debating with learned elders, despite the concern that this causes his parents.

These tales are there not simply to form the 'orderly account' that Luke promises (Luke 1:1, NRSV), but also, more importantly, to help create a growing awareness that the events surrounding Jesus' early years are deeply revealing of his mission and identity. At each significant moment, Luke seems to say, God is shaping Jesus' self-understanding of the work that he will carry out, setting his life in the context of the prophets who have gone before and alongside those whom he will redeem. And repeatedly, Luke offers explanation of how, through Christ, the whole world will be saved.

Jesus, in Luke's gospel, reflects God's especial mercy and love for the neglected, the poor and the despised. Repeatedly he calls them to hear and obey the word of God. He warns the arrogant and proud that if they do not change their ways, they will be lost. He teaches by means of parables, drawing out understanding and speaking with such authority that his critics are silenced. And he aligns himself repeatedly with the divine Spirit of wisdom and truth. Jesus is filled – as the prophets were – with the Spirit, but to a greater degree than the world has previously seen. He utilises all wisdom's gifts to share God's truth. And wisdom tells Jesus that for him, like many of the prophets and teachers of old, condemnation of hypocrisy, injustice and the abuse of power will lead towards persecution and death (Luke 11:49). His timeless wisdom is for us, too; may we be led to realise that we, through his guidance, have also 'increased in wisdom and in years' (Luke 2:52).

AMANDA BLOOR

Recognising salvation

Simeon took him in his arms and praised God, saying, 'Master, now you are dismissing your servant in peace, according to your word; for my eyes have seen your salvation, which you have prepared in the presence of all peoples, a light for revelation to the Gentiles and for glory to your people Israel.' And the child's father and mother were amazed at what was being said about him.

I wonder where you would look for God's revelation and salvation, or how you would recognise it. Simeon, who has been waiting in the temple to see the promised Messiah, has the wisdom to look beyond appearances. It is likely that he has been expecting the appearance of a warrior-king who will lead Israel's people to freedom, but instead he recognises the fulfilment of his hopes in the fragile body of a baby boy. Taking Jesus in his arms, he offers a spontaneous outpouring of thanksgiving and praise to God. It must have been a bittersweet moment for Simeon: the joy of revelation mixed with the painful realisation of his own mortality. God's promise that he would live until he had seen the Christ means that his own death must now be drawing near.

The story is a reminder for us that God comes to us in many ways and in many forms. The infant Jesus holds within himself all the potential that Simeon recognises. But more than that, he is already the embodied wisdom and power of God. Both divine and human, Jesus is truly God with us, in the heart of our messy, disordered lives, bringing promise and hope.

There is another reminder, too. God's wisdom is not only for the old! Simeon saw the promise of this particular, unique child, but God is able to work through the most apparently unlikely people, regardless of age, position or status. Perhaps God might even be working through you.

Gracious God, you guided Simeon to recognise your infant Son as his salvation and consolation. Help us to look for Christ's presence in those we meet today, and through him to draw closer to your presence.

AMANDA BLOOR

Testing times

Jesus, full of the Holy Spirit, returned from the Jordan and was led by the Spirit in the wilderness, where for forty days he was tempted by the devil. He ate nothing at all during those days, and when they were over, he was famished. The devil said to him, 'If you are the Son of God, command this stone to become a loaf of bread.' Jesus answered him, 'It is written, "One does not live by bread alone."'… When the devil had finished every test, he departed from him until an opportune time.

Freshly baptised, identified by God as 'beloved' and filled with the Holy Spirit, Jesus is faced in the wilderness with the reality of evil and the subtlety of desire. Fasting has left him famished, and his physical weakness would have been matched by mental exhaustion; it would have been simple to slip into behaviour that he would otherwise have recognised as foolish and wrong. Yet Jesus avoids this. Despite his hunger, he refuses to turn stones into bread. He looks down from a great height and avoids the suggestion to throw himself off in the hope that God's angels will lift him up. He clings to God and refuses to submit to temptation.

We might find ourselves faced with similar questions. Am I so hungry for something that I will do anything to possess it? Do I want recognition and power so much that I'm prepared to worship the person who can give it to me? And can I believe that God loves me without dramatically putting it to the test?

Jesus' great wisdom in this story is to know his own limitations. He gives himself completely into God's hands, because that is the only solution.

There is one other point to note. These are the great temptations, but they are not the end. The devil waits for 'an opportune time' (v. 13). Jesus will be tested again, as we all are. The struggle requires that we keep close to God, for God's is the only strength that lasts.

God, our strength and our shield, save us from falling into temptations that are too hard to withstand. Defend us from all evil, including our own disordered desires. Let us serve only you.

AMANDA BLOOR

Wisdom and authority

And he rolled up the scroll, gave it back to the attendant, and sat down. The eyes of all in the synagogue were fixed on him. Then he began to say to them, 'Today this scripture has been fulfilled in your hearing.' All spoke well of him and were amazed at the gracious words that came from his mouth. They said, 'Is this not Joseph's son?'… And he said, 'Truly I tell you, no prophet is accepted in the prophet's home town.'

We sometimes find wisdom where we least expect it. This is certainly true when Jesus begins his ministry. Travelling around Galilee and teaching in the synagogues, he is praised by those who hear him speak, that is, until he comes to his home town of Nazareth. After reading from the prophet Isaiah, Jesus begins to interpret the scriptures. At first, he is feted for his 'gracious words', but when he makes blunt comparisons between their surprise and the experiences of the prophets Elijah and Elisha, his listeners are outraged. They drive him out of town and threaten his life.

Jesus is, as ever, realistic about human nature. He knows that it is difficult to overcome people's expectations, especially if these are low. It's easier, somehow, to respect the views of a stranger than it is to recognise wisdom offered by a person whose everyday life is familiar to us. Perhaps it's because we find it hard to overlook apparent faults or weaknesses that might undermine their authority. Perhaps it's because we don't trust ourselves and so dismiss anyone who seems to be too similar to us. It's even harder to hear criticism from a neighbour or acquaintance. We suspect a hidden agenda and block out what might, in fact, be truth.

Might we have done the same if we had been in the synagogue listening to Jesus? Much as I hope I would have recognised his qualities, I know that I too might have dismissed the words of the carpenter's son. Recognising wisdom in others requires humility and the readiness to learn.

Let me not make assumptions, Lord. Give me the wisdom to know my own prejudices and a willingness to hear your truth in the mouths of others.

AMANDA BLOOR

What matters most

'Which is easier, to say, "Your sins are forgiven you", or to say, "Stand up and walk"? But so that you may know that the Son of Man has authority on earth to forgive sins' – he said to the one who was paralysed – 'I say to you, stand up and take your bed and go to your home.' Immediately he stood up before them, took what he had been lying on, and went to his home, glorifying God.

It's surprising that in this story it's the faith of his friends rather than the paralysed person himself that Christ praises. Their motivation isn't clear; they might have been hoping for a healing, or simply wanting their friend not to be left out, despite the fact that he wasn't able to push through the crowds being taught by the rabbi from Nazareth. They probably weren't expecting Jesus to notice them at all, let alone to offer their friend absolution.

By forgiving the man's sins, Jesus offends the Pharisees and teachers who are listening to him. They see this as blasphemy: 'Only God can forgive sins!' (Luke 5:21, CEB). Yet they are silenced by Jesus' response. It is undoubtedly easier to say 'You are forgiven' than it is to say 'Stand up and walk'. But only Jesus can do both. He demonstrates God's love by offering forgiveness, and he proves that this forgiveness is real by healing the body as well as the spirit.

It's wisdom on a very practical, human scale, demonstrating Jesus' psychological acuity as well as his power. He's ready to break off from abstract theological discussions with wise religious leaders in order to offer freedom from the false belief, prevalent at the time, that disability is the result of sin. He knows that kindness matters. He also watches what is happening on the fringes of the action. It's not only the paralysed man who is noticed; the friends who care for him are offered thanks and encouragement too. To Jesus, all people are of value and all deserve attention.

Jesus, help me to believe that you care for my well-being in body and spirit, and help me to treat others with compassion and respect.

AMANDA BLOOR

Lawful or right?

Then Jesus said to them, 'I ask you, is it lawful to do good or to do harm on the sabbath, to save life or to destroy it?' After looking around at all of them, he said to him, 'Stretch out your hand.' He did so, and his hand was restored. But they were filled with fury and discussed with one another what they might do to Jesus.

The law is clear, yet Jesus' instincts are not to retreat behind legalities, but rather to help and to heal. He knows that his opponents are keen to find reasons to accuse him of wrongdoing, but he is not to be dissuaded. He calls forward the man – this is to be a very public healing – and does in the full view of his enemies what he knows to be right, despite the likely consequences.

Luke sets this story immediately after a similar challenging of convention by Jesus' disciples, who hungrily gather grain to eat as they pass through a cornfield on another sabbath. When censured for the actions of his disciples, Jesus states openly that he is 'lord of the sabbath'.

Together, the two stories not only draw a direct line between David and Jesus, but they also explicitly reveal Jesus as being greater than David and his actions as being directed by God's wisdom and love, not by the law.

Each day we can find ourselves having to make choices about what we do and how we behave. Sometimes the choice is clearly between good and evil, but often it's more complex than that. Do the choices we make show that we are acting in a way that honours God and loves others? Are we taking time to care for ourselves as well as others, believing that we are God's much-loved children?

In this story, Jesus challenges us: can we recognise what matters most? The sabbath is a gift to us from God, rather than a means of control. Is it lawful to do good? Is it right?

Fill my heart with gratitude, Lord, for the gift of rest and refreshment;
make me always ready to recognise need and swift to do good.

AMANDA BLOOR

Discerning the good

'To what then will I compare the people of this generation, and what are they like?… For John the Baptist has come eating no bread and drinking no wine, and you say, "He has a demon"; the Son of Man has come eating and drinking, and you say, "Look, a glutton and a drunkard, a friend of tax-collectors and sinners!" Nevertheless, wisdom is vindicated by all her children.'

We live in a society that could be accused of operating a cult of personality. Electronic communications have made it easier than ever before to build up someone's public profile and then to knock it down again. It's often difficult to distinguish what is true from what is false or to seek a balanced viewpoint amid hype or extremism. Luke shows us that this is not a new problem. Jesus is talked about throughout Galilee; he has taught wisely, healed the sick and even raised the dead. He's caused a sensation! But some are still unsure. Perhaps, they think, they're being deceived by a charlatan or perhaps the reports are exaggerated or untrue. Even John the Baptist sends some of his disciples to find out if Jesus really is the one that they have all been waiting for.

Jesus responds with some disappointment. After all, he has worked tirelessly to bring good news and offer healing of mind and body. 'What do you see?' he challenges the crowds around him. 'What are you looking for? How can you get it so wrong?'

Judging by appearances can lead us astray. Whether we, like the crowds, see an ascetic and assume they have a mental illness, or see conviviality and criticise it as self-indulgence, it's very easy to look only at the surface rather than what lies beneath. Jesus, in this passage, asks us to do two things: to recognise him as wisdom and then to exercise wisdom ourselves, allowing God to work through and in us.

Loving God, fill me with your Spirit of divine wisdom, that I may be guided to see what is true, discern what is good and do what is right.

AMANDA BLOOR

Forgiveness and love

'You gave me no water for my feet, but she has bathed my feet with her tears and dried them with her hair. You gave me no kiss, but from the time I came in she has not stopped kissing my feet. You did not anoint my head with oil, but she has anointed my feet with ointment. Therefore, I tell you, her sins which were many, have been forgiven; hence she has shown great love. But the one to whom little is forgiven, loves little.'

The woman described by Luke in this story is emotionally and physically demonstrative towards Jesus. The Pharisee who has invited Jesus to eat at his house is offended by the scene, both because of the sensuous nature of the woman's actions and because she is a 'sinner' who should not be touching the honoured guest. Jesus, realising what is going through his mind, rebukes the man. 'Compare your welcome to me with hers,' he says.

It's easy to be swept up in the drama and misunderstand the point of Jesus' words. It is not because the woman has done this for Jesus that she is forgiven – he's not that shallow. It's precisely the opposite. Because Jesus has welcomed her, she wants to do what she can for the man who has shown her gentleness and respect. Jesus has acted towards her in the way that God, as Jesus teaches, acts to all who come in humility and trust; she in return overflows with love and gratitude.

Jesus' forgiveness of her 'many' sins sets the woman free to love without reservation. Her tears might show repentance for her past or joy for a future unburdened by guilt; we don't know and, really, it doesn't matter. Forgiveness allows her to show love, knowing that she is loved in return. It's a virtuous circle. Jesus' wisdom is shown in his understanding of what is necessary – he doesn't criticise or condemn – and his ability to receive the love of another. Can we, through God's help, do the same?

There are things in my life for which I'm sorry and ashamed, Lord.
Give me trust to draw close to you, loving you with my whole heart
and accepting your love in return.

AMANDA BLOOR

Practical wisdom

He did not allow anyone to enter with him, except Peter, John, and James, and the child's father and mother. They were all weeping and wailing for her; but he said, 'Do not weep; for she is not dead but sleeping.' And they laughed at him, knowing that she was dead. But he took her by the hand and called out, 'Child, get up!' Her spirit returned, and she got up at once. Then he directed them to give her something to eat.

This story, for me, is not only about a miraculous event, but also an example of Jesus' level-headed response to a crisis. Remaining calm, he ignores the scoffing of mourners and has the sensitivity to keep outsiders well away from what is a deeply private moment. This is a young girl, not a sideshow for the amazement of onlookers. Then, having commanded the child to rise from her bed, Jesus' first thought is for her most immediate needs; he insists that she is given something to eat. She's been through a lot and she'll be hungry. First things first.

It's easy to think that divine wisdom is all about abstract concepts and theological depth, but it's important to remember that practical issues may often have to come first. Jesus, our incarnate Saviour, knows this. We are bodily creatures, and we need to look after the body as well as the soul. There is little point in bringing the child back to health only for her to fade away from lack of nutrition! Jesus also realises that difficult moments need careful responses; his insistence on keeping the crowds away allows him to concentrate on what really needs to be done. I wonder if we have similar wisdom in tricky situations, or if we find ourselves distracted by a multitude of competing voices. Can we find peace enough to dig deep within ourselves, discover God-given resources, keep calm and act with confidence and clarity? Wisdom is a gift and a guide. Make space to listen and then to act.

Jesus, my hope and my life, help me not to panic when faced with disaster, but to think clearly, act prayerfully, do what is necessary and not be afraid.

AMANDA BLOOR

Friendship and support

After this the Lord appointed seventy others and sent them on ahead of him in pairs to every town and place where he himself intended to go. He said to them, 'The harvest is plentiful, but the labourers are few; therefore ask the Lord of the harvest to send out labourers into his harvest. Go on your way. See, I am sending you out like lambs into the midst of wolves.'

I'm sure that we can all think of times when we have felt like lambs in the middle of a pack of wolves – outnumbered, vulnerable and ill-prepared for the situation we've found ourselves in. Jesus already knows this, because since the beginning of his ministry he's faced human and spiritual opponents and has repeatedly had to deal with critics and enemies. His followers, however, are filled with the enthusiasm that can lead to naive optimism. There is a job to be done and they are keen to do it – but they need to be given support.

Jesus demonstrates a wise grasp of skills that are still relevant to Christian leadership today. He chooses a group of people who seem right for the task of bringing God's love to the local towns and villages. He gives them a plan of action, encouraging them to travel simply, accept hospitality, cure the sick and share God's peace. 'Don't take valuables with you,' he warns, 'and if you are not welcome, leave that place behind.' And, most importantly, he sends them out in pairs rather than alone.

Some of this guidance is to keep them as safe as possible. Without possessions they'll move swiftly and be less of a target for robbers. But Jesus also knows that if times are difficult or things go wrong, they'll need encouragement and support. Together, they can pray and keep a sense of balance. They'll know that they're not alone. And, sure enough, they return to him full of joy and confidence. Do we, like them, have a partner in our own mission or ministry?

Jesus, source of all authority and power, I long to be a labourer in your harvest. Give me good travelling companions and staunch friends so that I may return to you with joy.

AMANDA BLOOR

Don't worry; be ready

'Nothing is covered up that will not be uncovered, and nothing secret that will not become known… When they bring you before the synagogues, the rulers, and the authorities, do not worry about how you are to defend yourselves or what you are to say; for the Holy Spirit will teach you at that very hour what you ought to say.'

For a long time after I left school, a recurrent nightmare I had when I was stressed involved realising that I was about to take an exam on a subject for which I'd had no lessons and about which I knew absolutely nothing. I would wake in a complete panic and have to tell myself that school exams were well behind me! Most of us can remember times when we've been put under pressure, either in formal examinations or in situations like job interviews, and how stressful it can be to try to prepare adequately so that we perform well. Yet here is Jesus, open about the trials and difficulties that will face his disciples and telling them not to think ahead. 'Don't think about what you will say,' he tells them. 'Don't worry.'

Easier said than done, perhaps, especially after a warning that even whispered secrets will be shouted from the housetops by their enemies. But Jesus wants to reassure his followers that they are loved completely and absolutely by God. In whatever trials they face, they won't be alone. They will have the Holy Spirit, the comforter, to inspire and teach them. When they need words, they will find them.

It's a wisdom that has as much to say to us today as it did then. It's easy to become paralysed by inaction because of fear of getting things wrong, of looking foolish, of failing. Worry holds us back and keeps us in the shadows. But we are asked to step out in Christ's light, filled with the inspiration of the Holy Spirit. With God's help, we can be ready for anything.

Take away my fear, Lord; fill me with your courage and wisdom,
and teach me what to do and say.

AMANDA BLOOR

Living in the real world

So they watched him and sent spies who pretended to be honest, in order to trap him by what he said... But he perceived their craftiness and said to them, 'Show me a denarius. Whose head and whose title does it bear?' They said, 'The emperor's.' He said to them, 'Then give to the emperor the things that are the emperor's, and to God the things that are God's.' And they were not able in the presence of the people to trap him...

Jesus always grounds his actions in worldly as well as spiritual wisdom. Presented with an apparently innocuous question about religious observation and financial responsibilities, Jesus sees the trap straight away and refuses to fall into it. His answer neatly avoids standing on either side of the religious–civil divide and must have caused his opponents to question who it was they were sent to incriminate; he is not the naive and unworldly preacher they might have been expecting to meet, but a clever and quick thinker.

Jesus' response has something to say to us, too. As Christians, we live in the real world, where our beliefs and actions may be guided by our faith and conscience, but also must fit with the laws and understandings of the societies of which we are members. Doing so, despite the Judeo-Christian heritage that has shaped much of our legislation, isn't always easy. Jesus' words encourage us not to set ourselves apart, but to bring all that we are (including our faith) to the service of the world as well as to God. It may be necessary to be diplomats and politicians, so that we can act with both innocence and wisdom in our dealings with worldly matters!

As citizens of civil societies, we need to hold our leaders to account, but also to live with respect for the laws and customs of our land. We are called to live in ways that honour both God and humankind.

Gracious God, you made and love the world and everything in it. Give me wisdom to know what belongs to earthly powers and what is yours, and the generosity to give back what is due.

AMANDA BLOOR

Judges 1—12

During a weekly chat with two other writers, I bemoaned the drafting of these notes because of how hard the book of Judges can feel when God's people disobey him time after time. One of my friends said, 'Remember that this book was written at the same time as the book of Ruth! When we read the two together, we can cling to the grace we see in Ruth's story.' This insight strengthened me and helped me to retain some objectivity.

Reading this book can feel difficult. It comes at the end of Joshua's life, he who led the people into the promised land. But after he dies, the judges and the Israelites seem to descend into a spiral of disobedience when they don't completely inhabit the land of Canaan, as God told them to do. The judges become more and more of a negative influence the further into the book we read, with God's people turning from him readily. Even my understanding of Gideon, one of the best-known characters here, changed when I read his account this time. I used to think that perhaps he was very timid and in need of a lot of assurance, but then I realised how far Gideon seems from God, treating him as one would the other gods, such as Baal. It's not a pretty picture.

But there are pockets of hope amid the hard stories. For instance, we'll read one of the oldest poems in the Hebrew Bible, written by a woman who leads God's people when a man won't. We'll have a glimpse of hope when the Israelites repent, turning back to God. And in Gideon's story, we'll see God showing his glory through the victory over the Midianites with only 300 men in the fight.

I'm grateful for the help of various biblical commentators who increased my understanding of Judges, including K. Lawson Younger, Jr, *Judges and Ruth: NIV Application Commentary* (Zondervan, 2011), and, for the quotations from the church fathers, John R. Franke (ed.), *Ancient Christian Commentary on Scripture: Old Testament IV – Joshua, Judges, Ruth, 1–2 Samuel* (InterVarsity Press, 2005).

Are you ready to engage with this often-overlooked book of the Bible? Buckle your seatbelt; here we go!

AMY BOUCHER PYE

Obeying God fully

When they sent men to spy out Bethel (formerly called Luz), the spies saw a man coming out of the city and they said to him, 'Show us how to get into the city and we will see that you are treated well.' So he showed them, and they put the city to the sword but spared the man and his whole family. He then went to the land of the Hittites, where he built a city and called it Luz, which is its name to this day. But Manasseh did not drive out the people of Beth Shan or Taanach or Dor or Ibleam or Megiddo and their surrounding settlements, for the Canaanites were determined to live in that land.

The book of Judges opens with a major theme – God's people not following his commands completely. Although God's book of the law calls them to take possession of the promised land fully, they fail again and again. As we see in the text, they 'spared the man and his whole family' (v. 25) and they 'did not drive out' (v. 27) the various peoples. The Israelites lack obedience, which sends them further away from God as they become intertwined with the Canaanites. They repeatedly fail to follow God's commands, which corresponds to their decline as a people.

As people of today's world, we can find the routing of native peoples troublesome, to say the least. As we read this book of historical narrative, we do well to remember the original culture and context, and to understand that God is not calling nations to a special status as his people today as he did in the Old Testament.

What we can take away is an encouragement to obey God fully in our own lives, driving out any sinful practices that have wormed their way in. When we sense God's loving correction as we read the Bible, hear his still, small voice or receive a nudge of his Spirit through a loving friend, we should bend our wills to him. Then we will flourish in his kingdom.

'Jesus replied: "'Love the Lord your God with all your heart and with all your soul and with all your mind.' This is the first and greatest commandment"' (Matthew 22:37–38).

AMY BOUCHER PYE

The gift of tears

The angel of the Lord went up from Gilgal to Bokim and said, 'I brought you up out of Egypt and led you into the land that I swore to give to your ancestors. I said, "I will never break my covenant with you, and you shall not make a covenant with the people of this land, but you shall break down their altars." Yet you have disobeyed me. Why have you done this? And I have also said, "I will not drive them out before you; they will become traps for you, and their gods will become snares to you."' When the angel of the Lord had spoken these things to all the Israelites, the people wept aloud, and they called that place Bokim. There they offered sacrifices to the Lord.

I find tears fascinating, especially since learning that scientific researchers have discovered that tears shed in response to an emotional situation bring more healing to one's body than those cried at, for instance, the cutting of an onion. The emotional tears remove toxic substances not found in other types of tears. God has designed our bodies in amazing ways.

Tears can also be seen as a gift, especially when they signal a change in heart and a willingness to repent, such as the tearful response of the Israelites when God's messenger highlights their infidelity to him. God has saved them from the Egyptians, yet the Israelites go against his instructions and bind themselves to other peoples. But when confronted with the reality of their actions, and how the people of the land will become a trap for them, they turn from their actions. Their hearts are sensitive to God, and they still want to follow him.

When we allow ourselves to release pent-up emotions through a tearful response, we may be led into a place of healing. Certainly we know that God will hear our prayers and forgive us of our wrongdoings.

Father God, we have sinned against you in thought, word and deed.
Make our hearts pliable, that we might return to you as soon as we begin
to stray. May we know the gift of tears and your forgiveness.

AMY BOUCHER PYE

For our benefit

After Joshua had dismissed the Israelites, they went to take possession of the land, each to their own inheritance. The people served the Lord throughout the lifetime of Joshua and of the elders who outlived him and who had seen all the great things the Lord had done for Israel... After that whole generation had been gathered to their ancestors, another generation grew up who knew neither the Lord nor what he had done for Israel. Then the Israelites did evil in the eyes of the Lord and served the Baals. They forsook the Lord, the God of their ancestors, who had brought them out of Egypt. They followed and worshipped various gods of the peoples around them.

Those in the early church saw Joshua as a type of Christ, for the Hebrew name Joshua is Jesus in Greek. Joshua delivered God's people into the promised land and, after he died, they had a choice. Would they serve God or other gods? Would they become captive to sin or would they embrace the freedom God gave them to love him?

These questions concerned Origen, a third-century scholar in the Greek church, who is often seen as one of the most important early theologians. In his homilies on Judges, he noted that when the Israelites serve God, they escape being delivered into the hands of plunderers. But when they serve their own passions, they are given over to them. Thus, Origen concludes, God's rules are for his people; God wrote them for our sakes, and not to harm us.

Reframing the reading of the law in this light can change our understanding of what can seem stark and even harsh rules. God wants his people not to perish, but to flourish. His laws are a means of promoting life and liberty.

May we embrace God's standards for our lives as we live to honour him.

'Who will rescue me from this body that is subject to death?
Thanks be to God, who delivers me through Jesus Christ our Lord!
So then, I myself in my mind am a slave to God's law, but in my sinful
nature a slave to the law of sin' (Romans 7:24–25).

AMY BOUCHER PYE

God's representatives

Then the Lord raised up judges, who saved them out of the hands of these raiders. Yet they would not listen to their judges but prostituted themselves to other gods and worshipped them. They quickly turned from the ways of their ancestors, who had been obedient to the Lord's commands. Whenever the Lord raised up a judge for them, he was with the judge and saved them out of the hands of their enemies as long as the judge lived; for the Lord relented because of their groaning under those who oppressed and afflicted them. But when the judge died, the people returned to ways even more corrupt than those of their ancestors.

When we hear that God raised up judges, we might think of people who decide on important matters, in line with the English meaning of the word. But the Hebrew word implies those who adopted a role of saving, or rescuing, God's people. God knew that his people would continue to turn from him, slipping into a life of disobedience and wrongdoing. So he sent his representatives to do his work. Does that sound familiar?

Yes, it's God's story of redemption, which we see not only in the Old Testament but also in the New, when God sends his Son Jesus to save us from our sins. The judges we see here, however, are not perfect, like Jesus. Some do good; some do not; and some do a mix of good and evil.

But the people are better off with a judge over them, for although they soon disobey God, a judge delivers them from the hands of their oppressors. Although the Israelites think they know what is best for their lives, they need rescuing.

We may easily fall into the sin of pride when life seems to be going well and we're thriving in various areas. But when we face challenges, we might more easily turn to God for help and comfort. Perhaps we can ask God to so infuse our lives that we will turn to him at all times, as we give thanks for our rescuer, Jesus.

Lord Jesus Christ, Son of the living God, have mercy on me, a sinner.

AMY BOUCHER PYE

Killing the king

Again the Israelites cried out to the Lord, and he gave them a deliverer – Ehud, a left-handed man, the son of Gera the Benjaminite... [Ehud] said, 'Your majesty, I have a secret message for you.' The king said to his attendants, 'Leave us!' And they all left. Ehud then approached him while he was sitting alone in the upper room of his palace and said, 'I have a message from God for you.' As the king rose from his seat, Ehud reached with his left hand, drew the sword from his right thigh and plunged it into the king's belly... While they waited, Ehud got away. He passed by the stone images and escaped to Seirah... That day Moab was made subject to Israel, and the land had peace for eighty years.

The unabridged version of this story contains many vivid, and unpleasant, details. For this saviour of God's people – this judge – is a man who employs deception in his actions. Yet God uses him to usher in 80 years of peace. As St Augustine notes, that is twice as long as the peace that even King Solomon reigned over.

While the story of Ehud and his killing of the king is graphic, it also contains a certain level of satire – namely that the courtiers are so under the influence of their king that they don't investigate what is happening in the locked chamber, thinking that he is taking his time to relieve himself. The smell of the discharge of the king's bowels as he died probably adds to the courtiers' misunderstanding.

We see in this story how God can use the just and the unjust as he puts his kingdom into place. He didn't cause Ehud to kill the king, but he redeemed this violence for the benefit of his people.

This is another hard passage, admittedly. Take some moments to reflect on what you read, and what you think about it.

Father God, we often don't understand all that has happened in the past, or why. Bring us understanding, that we might grow in wisdom and stature.

AMY BOUCHER PYE

The weak made strong

Now Deborah, a prophet, the wife of Lappidoth, was leading Israel at that time… She sent for Barak… and said to him, 'The Lord, the God of Israel, commands you: "Go, take with you ten thousand men… and lead them up to Mount Tabor. I will lead Sisera… with his chariots and his troops to the River Kishon and give him into your hands."' Barak said to her, 'If you go with me, I will go; but if you don't go with me, I won't go.' 'Certainly I will go with you,' said Deborah. 'But because of the course you are taking, the honour will not be yours, for the Lord will deliver Sisera into the hands of a woman.'

Debates over the leadership of women in the church have raged over the centuries. Ambrose, the bishop of Milan in the fourth century and an influential church leader, said of Deborah, the first female judge, in 'Concerning Widows': 'I think that her judgeship has been narrated and her deeds described, that women should not be restrained from deeds of valour by the weakness of their sex. A widow, she governs the people; a widow, she leads armies; a widow, she chooses generals; a widow, she determines wars and orders triumphs. So, then, it is not… sex but valour which makes strong.'

Valour and obedience to God's commands she had. She was a prophet and a leader in a patriarchal society. Deborah was used by God for his glory, for she was not the obvious person to lead his people from their oppressors. Note her faith in God when she tells Barak what course of action to take while saying what she'll do – she is speaking on behalf of 'the Lord, the God of Israel' (v. 6).

God can use the strong and the weak to fulfil his purposes in the world. May we join Deborah in believing that he is able to accomplish more than we could ask or imagine.

Lord God, you are keenly interested in the world you created,
and the people you've made. Increase our faith, that we may believe
that you will act for good in our world.

AMY BOUCHER PYE

A song of victory

On that day Deborah and Barak son of Abinoam sang this song: 'When the princes in Israel take the lead, when the people willingly offer themselves – praise the Lord! Hear this, you kings! Listen, you rulers! I, even I, will sing to the Lord; I will praise the Lord, the God of Israel, in song. When you, Lord, went out from Seir, when you marched from the land of Edom, the earth shook, the heavens poured, the clouds poured down water. The mountains quaked before the Lord, the One of Sinai, before the Lord, the God of Israel.'

Do you enjoy reading or writing poetry? Of late I've been incorporating poetry into my times of engaging with the Bible. Each day I'll take a small portion of scripture and turn it into a poem. I find that taking the time to play around with the words makes me slow down and helps me to digest the passage, often moving me from an intellectual response to a more heartfelt one.

Deborah's song captures in five acts the victory over Sisera that we read about yesterday in prose. Scholars believe that Deborah's song may be one of the oldest pieces of writing in the Hebrew Bible, but they disagree over its themes, authorship, structure and unity. Throughout its five acts Deborah narrows her focus, starting with the nation of Israel as a whole, then moving to individual tribes, and then finally to two women. It's complex, but at its heart she gives glory to God for his leadership in their victory. She acknowledges that earthly kings and rulers should bow to the Lord of all, he who shakes the earth and parts the clouds (v. 4).

Why not take some time this weekend to put a biblical text into a poetic form? You don't have to share it with anyone, but you can use it for your own enrichment. I hope you are surprised and delighted at how God meets you through this exercise.

Lord God, you are the creator of all, and you've made us in your image. Help us to embrace whatever forms of creativity we are most comfortable with this day, for our benefit and your glory.

AMY BOUCHER PYE

Testing God

Gideon said to God, 'If you will save Israel by my hand as you have promised – look, I will place a wool fleece on the threshing-floor. If there is dew only on the fleece and all the ground is dry, then I will know that you will save Israel by my hand, as you said.' And that is what happened. Gideon rose early the next day; he squeezed the fleece and wrung out the dew – a bowlful of water. Then Gideon said to God, 'Do not be angry with me. Let me make just one more request. Allow me one more test with the fleece, but this time make the fleece dry and let the ground be covered with dew.' That night God did so. Only the fleece was dry; all the ground was covered with dew.

Many Christians know the story of Gideon and his fleeces, often seeing it as a means of discerning God's will. Yet if we read the story in its wider context, we understand that Gideon's tests reveal more about his lack of faith rather than pointing towards a fruitful means of hearing God. After all, the Lord has already assured Gideon that he will deliver the Midianites to him, which Gideon repeats when asking for the first confirmation: 'as you have promised' (v. 36).

Instead, Gideon through his fear continues to test God, more along the lines of how one would speak to Baal or other gods, rather than to Yahweh. In fact, Gideon often uses a generic Hebrew word for God rather than addressing him as Yahweh, the term that denotes the God of the Israelites. But through his grace, God answers Gideon with the wet and dry fleece. Yet, as we will see tomorrow, the Lord will take measures to ensure that all the glory of the victory over the Midianites is returned to him.

When we seek a close relationship with God, we can ask for confirmation and help when we need wisdom and understanding. But this story seems to warn against trying, from a distance, to manipulate God.

Lord God, you answer me when I call. Help me to trust you completely, knowing that you seek what is good for me, that I might bring you honour and praise.

AMY BOUCHER PYE

For whom?

The Midianites, the Amalekites and all the other eastern peoples had settled in the valley, thick as locusts. Their camels could no more be counted than the sand on the seashore. Gideon arrived just as a man was telling a friend his dream… His friend responded, 'This can be nothing other than the sword of Gideon son of Joash, the Israelite. God has given the Midianites and the whole camp into his hands.' When Gideon heard the dream and its interpretation, he bowed down and worshipped. He returned to the camp of Israel and called out, 'Get up!… When I and all who are with me blow our trumpets, then from all round the camp blow yours and shout, "For the Lord and for Gideon."'

Gideon yet again needs reassurance from God that he will follow through on his promises. He receives it when he overhears an enemy recounting a dream, and he worships God, the last time this book notes him doing so. Although he goes forward in faith, Gideon yet seeks some of the glory of the win, for he asks the men to shout, 'For the Lord and *for Gideon*' (v. 18, emphasis mine).

Although God doesn't abhor people with mixed motives, he longs that they would turn their allegiance to him fully. After the many tests that Gideon put the Lord through, we'd think that he'd be fully convinced that God would be behind the defeat of so many – those 'thick as locusts' – but unfortunately that's not the case. Rather, Gideon longs for a slice of the adulation.

I think, in contrast, of a man I know who works tirelessly to advance the kingdom of God while not worrying about who receives the credit. If he can draft some bullet points for a speech or article that someone else will write, he is happy to do so. Could I? Could you?

'Shout for joy to God, all the earth! Sing the glory of his name; make his praise glorious. Say to God, "How awesome are your deeds!… All the earth bows down to you; they sing praise to you, they sing the praises of your name"' (Psalm 66:1–4).

AMY BOUCHER PYE

True rule

The Israelites said to Gideon, 'Rule over us – you, your son and your grandson – because you have saved us from the hand of Midian.' But Gideon told them, 'I will not rule over you, nor will my son rule over you. The Lord will rule over you.' And he said, 'I do have one request, that each of you give me an earring from your share of the plunder.'... They answered, 'We'll be glad to give them.'... Gideon made the gold into an ephod, which he placed in Ophrah, his town. All Israel prostituted themselves by worshipping it there, and it became a snare to Gideon and his family.

'Do as I say and not as I do.' The quip might be made in jest, but we quickly realise its accuracy, for it's easier to imitate one's actions than one's words. Gideon shows some of this hypocrisy when he says, 'the Lord will rule over you,' for he continues as an unofficial leader, doing more than simply following God's lead. He also assumes the task of a priest when he creates the ephod. But he warps the priestly role, for instead of installing the ephod in the temple for the worship of God, he places it in his home town, as a glorification of himself. And 'all Israel prostituted themselves by worshipping it there' – they followed Gideon's lead in not praising the one and true God (v. 27).

We're all prone to self-deception, and that's why we need some gentle and loving truth-tellers in our lives. A few friends play this role for me. When I am ranting about something, they may question what underlying issues I might need to address – some that I have caused. I know I need people who will love me enough to speak the truth.

Gideon wasn't the hero of faith we might wish he could have been, but God used him all the same. Why not reflect on his story, which we've read over the past few days, and ponder what strikes you most from it.

Lord God, we often fail you, sometimes in ways we do not even realise.
Through your Holy Spirit, prompt us when we need correction
and keep us open to your love.

AMY BOUCHER PYE

Truth-telling in an age of lies

When Jotham was told about this, he climbed up on the top of Mount Gerizim and shouted to them, 'Listen to me, citizens of Shechem, so that God may listen to you… Have you acted honourably and in good faith by making Abimelek king? Have you been fair to Jerub-Baal and his family?… Remember that my father fought for you and risked his life to rescue you from the hand of Midian. But today you have revolted against my father's family. You have murdered his seventy sons on a single stone and have made Abimelek, the son of his female slave, king over the citizens of Shechem… So have you acted honourably and in good faith towards Jerub-Baal and his family today?… If you have not, let fire come out from Abimelek and consume you… and consume Abimelek!'

The failure of Gideon (here called Jerub-Baal) to serve the Lord whole-heartedly left his descendants in a mess, not least because he availed himself of many wives and concubines, contrary to the laws of Deuteronomy. The majority of his 70 sons perished at the hands of their half-brother, Abimelek, through this son's twisted means of ascending to the throne. He enlisted his mother's family to kill his father's sons and thus was crowned king over Shechem.

But the lone remaining brother, Jotham, tells a fable to prick the con-sciences of God's people while posing pointed questions to them. Will they act honourably? If not, he asks that they would be cursed – they and Abimelek. And that's what happens when Abimelek dies at the hand of a woman by a single stone – just as he killed the 70 brothers with a single stone.

The glimpses of hope in this story are few, but even in times of debauchery, one man was willing to speak the truth – even if immediately after doing so he fled out of fear. May we too be those who name the truth in an age of fake news.

'Let us hold unswervingly to the hope we profess, for he who promised is faithful. And let us consider how we may spur one another on towards love and good deeds' (Hebrews 10:23–24).

AMY BOUCHER PYE

Following other gods

Then the Israelites cried out to the Lord, 'We have sinned against you, forsaking our God and serving the Baals.' The Lord replied, 'When the Egyptians, the Amorites, the Ammonites, the Philistines, the Sidonians, the Amalekites and the Maonites oppressed you and you cried to me for help, did I not save you from their hands? But you have forsaken me and served other gods, so I will no longer save you. Go and cry out to the gods you have chosen. Let them save you when you are in trouble!' But the Israelites said to the Lord, 'We have sinned. Do with us whatever you think best, but please rescue us now.' Then they got rid of the foreign gods among them and served the Lord. And he could bear Israel's misery no longer.

'Lord, forgive me for what I am about to do.' Can you relate to that adage, which has echoes of Augustine of Hippo's cry in *Confessions* (in updated language): 'Lord, make me pure, but not yet'?

The Israelites seem to employ this sense of wanting God's forgiveness but not wanting to change. Again and again in the book of Judges, we see them turn from the true and living God as they pursue and honour other gods. The Lord responds with some frustration at his people's manipulations, telling them to go and get those other gods to save them.

We might want to take hope from the line 'And he could bear Israel's misery no longer' – but the compassion we might read into the English translation is less evident in the Hebrew. Rather, the original language conveys a sense of the Lord boiling up in frustration and anger with his people.

As I mentioned in the introduction, the book of Judges is set at the same time as the book of Ruth, so if we despair at the increasing waywardness of God's people, we can also take comfort in his tender care there.

Father God, may you pour out your mercy and grace on your people, for we are prone to chase after the things that bring us instant satisfaction. Quench our thirst with your living water.

AMY BOUCHER PYE

An unholy vow

And Jephthah made a vow to the Lord: 'If you give the Ammonites into my hands, whatever comes out of the door of my house to meet me when I return in triumph from the Ammonites will be the Lord's, and I will sacrifice it as a burnt offering.' Then Jephthah went over to fight the Ammonites, and the Lord gave them into his hands… When Jephthah returned to his home in Mizpah, who should come out to meet him but his daughter, dancing to the sound of tambourines! She was an only child… When he saw her, he tore his clothes and cried, 'Oh no, my daughter! You have brought me down and I am devastated. I have made a vow to the Lord that I cannot break.'

We read this story with downcast hearts, for Jephthah follows through on his vow and sacrifices his daughter. The biblical narrative doesn't comment on the wisdom of his making this promise in the first place, instead leaving the reader to decide on its foolishness. It's a passage that has been debated throughout the centuries, with Augustine noting in *Questions on Judges* the division it can bring between those who 'genuinely seek to know' what it means and those who 'oppose the Holy Scriptures' and assume that God delights in human sacrifice.

Reading the New Testament, I don't believe that God enjoys human sacrifice, but he honours his Son, who gives his life to wipe away the mark of humanity's disobedience. As Jephthah wept over making his vow, which meant his daughter would die, perhaps too the Lord regretted humanity's disobedience, which meant the death of his Son.

As we consider this difficult story, perhaps a point to ponder is how we use our words, and especially how we can stop and think before we make unwise promises or vows. I can only imagine the sorrow Jephthah must have experienced when, buoyed by the victory he had enacted with the Lord's help, he saw his daughter come out to greet him upon his return home.

---

*'It is a trap to dedicate something rashly and only later
to consider one's vows' (Proverbs 20:25).*

AMY BOUCHER PYE

Family fighting

The Ephraimite forces were called out, and they crossed over to Zaphon. They said to Jephthah, 'Why did you go to fight the Ammonites without calling us to go with you? We're going to burn down your house over your head.' Jephthah answered, 'I and my people were engaged in a great struggle with the Ammonites, and although I called, you didn't save me out of their hands. When I saw that you wouldn't help, I took my life in my hands and crossed over to fight the Ammonites, and the Lord gave me the victory over them. Now why have you come up today to fight me?'

Fighting within a family incites destruction. Whether sibling rivalry, children pitted against their parents or other relationships at odds, there are no winners. Long-time feuds have started over harsh words spoken in a family, and reconciliation can be slow or might not ever come.

We see intra-family fighting on a grander scale in this, the last text we're reading from the book of Judges. Perhaps Jephthah never got over the rejection he endured at the hands of his half-brothers, who drove him out of his home. He was probably still stinging from sacrificing his own daughter, as we saw yesterday. So when the Ephraimite forces ask him why he didn't employ them in the fight against the Ammonites, he responds with fighting words – and fighting actions that result in the death of 42,000 Ephraimites.

We can read this story, as many of those in these first chapters of Judges, as a cautionary tale. Although we can never change the thoughts or actions of another person, we can, with God's help, address our own sinful hearts. We can ask him to help us with the conflicts we face in our families, that he might help us, when possible, to promote peace and unity.

May we be those who bow before the almighty Lord in humility, welcoming him to work in and through us in our daily lives.

Father, Son and Holy Spirit, take what I've learned and gained from reading your word and plant it deep within me, that I might bear fruit.

AMY BOUCHER PYE

Songs of praise

'Singing belongs to one who loves,' Augustine is quoted as saying. Certainly singing expresses deep emotion, and love has been one of its main inspirations. Hymns express praise for God and love and concern for neighbour and planet.

I'm a keen singer. I've been in several choirs over the years, particularly with classical repertoires. I also sing in our church's worship group. Preparing for a concert is a combined effort as we rehearse together, working to understand and convey the meaning of the music. 'St Matthew's Passion', for example, is intensely personal, but it also enables the audience to participate – this isn't just a drama we watch without being involved; the choir meditates on Christ's betrayal, execution and promise of resurrection, events they witness on behalf of the hearer.

A hymn is similar but different. There's much less time to rehearse, so hymns are usually quite familiar or easy to learn. They allow participation in the service, which otherwise might become quite wordy and heavy. A tune makes participation much easier. We sing them with others, so we have to listen, too, follow the tune and create something new. Most importantly, they are sung to worship God.

Singing uses the whole body. See how aware you can be of the effect on your body, because the whole of you responds to the breath and the song. It is with the whole body that we participate in worship. For me, a good hymn engages the brain too. Poetry and symbolism don't just illustrate theology but become part of the spirituality and worship of the hymn. We employ 'hearts and minds and hands and voices in our choicest psalmody'.

Hymns challenge as well as console. Iona hymns might express anger at injustice or sorrow at suffering – surely there's a need for that in a service. Hymns can use human imagery for God or be more abstract, attempting to reach the transcendent.

Hymns have had long journeys to reach us. Some are composed like poems. Others go through many alterations over time, almost like folk songs; verses are added or lost. Fashions change, as does language. Some refer directly to the Bible; some may be more indirectly inspired. The following selection are only a few of those that I love to sing.

HARRY SMART

Let all things their creator bless

Let the sea resound, and all that is in it. Let the fields be jubilant, and everything in them; let all the trees of the forest sing for joy. Let all creation rejoice before the Lord, for he comes, he comes to judge the earth. He will judge the world in righteousness...

Dear Mother Earth, who day by day
Unfoldest blessings on our way,
O praise him, Alleluia!
The flowers and fruits that in thee grow,
Let them his glory also show.

The year 2018 was a significant birthday for me, and my wife and I went walking in the area around Assisi, a long-held 'bucket list' desire. It is beautiful but harsh and rugged countryside, and at its centre is a high mountain on whose slopes forests rise.

Francis of Assisi walked that rough terrain regularly, and I felt so close to him as we visited hermitages he would have known, including one in a gully on the mountainside, with a small cell where he slept. Nearby is a tree dated to his lifetime, which is reputedly where he preached to the birds.

Francis wrote many prayers and hymns. His 'Canticle of the Creatures' is the origin of the hymn 'All Creatures of our God and King', paraphrased by William Draper (the extract above is verse four). It shows the joy Francis felt in creation and his respect for it. His writings were inspired by the many biblical passages about creation, particularly the psalms and canticles, but including others such as the wonderful final chapters of Job.

Singing this hymn, we can join in with Francis' exuberance. His material simplicity, quite challenging even in its own time, allowed him to be free to praise God alongside the natural world around him. Perhaps it allowed him too to write the verse about death with greater openness and welcome than we normally encounter.

Francis said, 'If you exclude any of God's creatures from the shelter of compassion and pity, you will deal likewise with your fellow men.' How can our prayers and our services celebrate nature as Francis did?

HARRY SMART

Praise in many languages

'Who has cut a channel for the torrents of rain, and a way for the thunderbolt, to bring rain on a land where no one lives, on the desert, which is empty of human life, to satisfy the waste and desolate land, and to make the ground put forth grass?'

O Lord my God, when I in awesome wonder
Consider all the works thy hand hath made,
I see the stars, I hear the rolling thunder,
Thy power throughout the universe displayed:

Then sings my soul, my Saviour God, to thee:
How great thou art, how great thou art.

This hymn originated in the 1880s in the experience of a Swedish minister, Carl Boberg, as he was walking in the mountains during a thunderstorm. Others later added more verses. An English missionary, Stuart K. Hine, heard Russian Christians praying in the 1920s and added the third verse – 'And when I think that God, his Son not sparing, sent him to die, I scarce can take it in.' Hine later worked with Eastern European refugees fleeing the Nazi invasion during World War II, and this inspired the longing in the fourth verse – it is a heavenly and earthly home the singers yearn for.

While some hymns are solo compositions, 'How Great Thou Art' brings together the experiences of many – the awesomeness of nature; the exiles longing for home; the realisation of God's greatness. We are touched to the core by these experiences as Christians. Often our initial spiritual awakening is at the overwhelming grandeur of nature, and this hymn expresses that powerfully, linking it with the greatness of God's actions. Looking across from Iona to Mull on a moonlit night was a special one of mine. History, personal faith and creation spoke of God.

When I hear a colleague of mine, an amateur astronomer, talk about the distant nebulae he photographs, I have a sense of the hugely creative power of God. Surely the God who counts the sparrows and the stars is there for me, too, and is my ultimate home.

When did I last stop to consider God's work in nature?

HARRY SMART

When we were still far off

'So he set off and went to his father. But while he was still far off, his father saw him and was filled with compassion; he ran and put his arms around him and kissed him. Then the son said to him, "Father, I have sinned against heaven and before you; I am no longer worthy to be called your son." But the father said to his slaves, "Quickly, bring out a robe – the best one – and put it on him."'

There's a wideness in God's mercy, like the wideness of the sea.
There's a kindness in his justice, which is more than liberty.

Frederick W. Faber, the author of this hymn, was a 19th-century clergy-man who converted to Catholicism. He founded a community, the Wilfridians, which was later headed by Cardinal Newman. Faber struggled greatly with his relationship with the church in his early years, and his physical health was plagued by Bright's disease, a kidney illness.

There are no direct biblical quotations in this hymn, but the themes of redemption and a love that exceeds our fears run throughout. The hymn has been significantly edited over the years, losing several verses. I've come to realise how many hymns are altered or adapted – these aren't the same as hymns written as one piece by a named poet. Faber's hymn first appeared in a Catholic hymnal in 1854 and in 1933 in *The United Methodist Hymnal*. It originally began, 'Souls of men, why will you scatter, like a crowd of frightened sheep?' Our fear is that we are beyond reach and yet 'the love of God is broader than the scope of human mind'.

The beginning of the hymn as we know it focuses on our lack of comprehension of the scope of God's mercy for us. This is the good news that the prodigal son wanted first to challenge and then couldn't quite credit. The father's forgiveness is greater than the son imagined. 'There is plentiful redemption in the blood that has been shed,' Faber reminds us.

God is 'most wonderfully kind', we are assured in the last verse.
Can we 'take him at his word' by loving God more simply?

HARRY SMART

Physical and spiritual

Peter, bound with two chains, was sleeping between two soldiers, while guards in front of the door were keeping watch… Suddenly an angel of the Lord appeared… tapped Peter on the side and woke him, saying, 'Get up quickly.' And the chains fell off his wrists.

Long my imprisoned spirit lay
Fast bound in sin and nature's night;
Thine eye diffused a quickening ray,
I woke, the dungeon flamed with light;
My chains fell off, my heart was free,
I rose, went forth and followed thee.

This hymn is folksy, full of energy, tackling big theological concepts. Its liveliness reflects the freedom of which Charles Wesley writes. We repeat the last lines, chorusing, 'My chains fell off.' The relief is palpable. Peter's escape occurs as the church faces famine and Herod's persecution.

Chains can be psychological, spiritual or political. I worked for a packing company that used bullying management techniques, cared little for safety and relied on the fear of unemployment. I was able to return to university; for others it was their only opportunity for work. On a different scale, Wesley wrote of seeing a black slave woman beaten horrendously for overfilling a cup of tea. He preached and wrote against slavery.

Often patients facing serious illness will say to me, 'I've not done anything terrible in my life. I'm not a murderer, but I'm not perfect.' Most of us are in that position. We can feel imprisoned by our inadequacy as well as our active wrongdoing. We need to try to live differently, with respect and care for our environment and for the consequences of our lives upon others. Living simply and consuming less extravagantly seem to be key to this. But we sense that we can't free ourselves on our own.

Christianity allows neither the escapist dream of perfectionism nor the despair of amorality. We are freed by God's love for us, so that we don't become legalists or those who are driven by fear. We, alongside the rest of 'Adam's helpless race', are freed to be led and judged by love.

How should I live, knowing that my chains have fallen away?

HARRY SMART

Will you come and follow me?

'I… will take you to myself, so that where I am, there you may be also. And you know the way to the place where I am going.' Thomas said to him, 'Lord, we do not know where you are going. How can we know the way?' Jesus said to him, 'I am the way, and the truth, and the life.'

> *Come, my way, my truth, my life:*
> *Such a way as gives us breath;*
> *Such a truth as ends all strife;*
> *Such a life as conquers death…*
>
> *Come, my joy, my love, my heart:*
> *Such a joy as none can move.*

George Herbert (1593–1633), who wrote this hymn, was MP for Montgomery and later an Anglican priest near Salisbury. A friend of John Donne, who was also a clergyman and poet, Herbert was devoted to his parish and parishioners and was a keen musician.

The metaphysical poets tend to take some interesting stances on their subjects, whether these are religious or secular, as Donne's often seem on first reading. Herbert uses the language of love poetry in works such as 'Love III': 'Love bade me welcome'.

'The Call' is certainly a love poem. It is the disciple responding to the declaration Jesus makes. In John 14, Jesus is calling us. In Herbert's poem, the poet is calling on Jesus with new titles. The way has become internalised. We call on Christ to be our way, our light, our joy, as Herbert reflects on the path ahead.

In the third verse we call, 'Come, my joy, my love, my heart.' The way has become the heart that we follow – a heart of flesh and not of stone, perhaps, one which rejoices in God's love for us and our love for God. This is passionate stuff leading us along the path of Herbert's relationship with God so that we become travellers on the way too. We are sustained by the feast that 'mends in length' – that gets better and better.

Herbert's path wasn't always clear, and he was very aware of his own failings. How does 'The Call' help us to respond to Jesus?

HARRY SMART

The banquet and the guests

'The glory that you have given me I have given them, so that they may be one, as we are one, I in them and you in me, that they may become completely one, so that the world may know that you have sent me.'

O thou who at thy Eucharist didst pray
That all thy church should be for ever one,
Grant us at every Eucharist to say
With longing heart and soul, 'thy will be done':
O may we all one bread, one body be
Through this blest sacrament of unity…

We pray thee too for wanderers from thy fold;
O bring them back, good Shepherd of the sheep,
Back to the faith which saints believed of old.

One of the lovely aspects of being a hospital chaplain is working with people of different denominations and faiths. I'm Anglican, but I regularly visit Methodist patients, whose tradition is strong here in Lincolnshire. I have good relations with the Catholic community and am available for people of all faiths and none. It is need that comes first.

This hymn is usually sung at the most solemn moment of the Eucharist, as communicants go forward to the altar rail. It expresses the deep desire for unity and looks back to Christ's sharing of himself, drawing us together with those at that first last supper and with Christians since who have celebrated it. William Turton, the author, is thinking beyond the working together of different churches to the coming together of generations across time in the praise of God. Time and space are united.

As individuals and institutions, both wonderful and flawed, our unity isn't fully realised. We struggle with unity, often putting our own interests above those of the community and then achieving less than if we had worked together. The imagery of Eucharist expresses the call to overcome those tendencies towards division. How can we work to bring people together without insisting that they are made in our image?

Lord, help me to remember that there are many guests at your feast.

HARRY SMART

Deo gratias

Praise the Lord, my soul; all my inmost being, praise his holy name. Praise the Lord, my soul, and forget not all his benefits – who forgives all your sins and heals all your diseases.

Now thank we all our God
With heart and hands and voices,
Who wondrous things hath done,
In whom his world rejoices;
Who from our mother's arms
Hath blessed us on our way.

Martin Rinkart (1586–1649) wrote this in the midst of the Thirty Years War, throughout which his home town was occupied by different armies. Eilenburg sheltered war refugees and then suffered pestilence and the loss of most of its young male population. Rinkart presided over several thousand funerals, including that of his wife. He himself survived. When harsh taxes were imposed, Rinkart persuaded the occupiers to reduce them. During all this, he wrote a hymn of thanksgiving.

I often visit patients who have been through so much, mentally or physically, sometimes on a scale that is hard to fathom. I could never encourage someone to 'count your blessings' in such circumstances. But some, many in fact, manage to live with a sense of God's love for them, of the beauty of life, with a thankfulness that transcends the suffering they are going through.

Most of us have known something of God's love – a friend, parent, neighbour or someone else who has shown us care, love and respect. It can be like water to a dry seed, bringing life to us, and in response we begin to see other instances of kindness and of God's purpose for us. We will know times when we are perplexed, overwhelmed by 'ills'. Rinkart doesn't ask us to be without troubles, but to be freed from them. He encourages thankfulness and bravery in the face of adversity, but uses gentle, kind words.

At the end of the Thirty Years War, as the peace treaty was signed, this hymn was sung. Imagine that!

Can I allow myself to give thanks to God for all that he has done?

HARRY SMART

Resilience

If you listen carefully to the media you will know that resilience is a buzz-word. You will hear it in many different contexts, from sport to politics to economics. You may also become aware that Christians talk about it a lot as well.

The word 'resilience' comes from the Latin word *resilio*, which means to rebound or to spring back. In engineering, resilience describes the way some materials can recover their shape after having been under great pressure. More recently it has been used in psychology to describe the resilience of the human spirit – the way people recover from stress and cope with adversity. It is a quality that can be shown by individuals or whole communities as they adjust to difficult circumstances.

There is some debate as to how we become resilient. While we are born with a degree of resilience (think about a premature baby fighting for its life), we can also develop resilience as we go through life, learning from the challenges we face how to persevere and keep going. This means that resilience can be enhanced or increased through learning, and there is now a growing interest in identifying the factors that make for resilience, both in children and adults.

While the Bible does not use the word 'resilience', it does record many examples of people who showed great resilience in their lives, and we can learn from their examples – think about the men and women of faith listed in Hebrews 11. The nearest equivalent word for resilience in scripture is the Greek word *hupomone*, usually translated as 'perseverance' or 'endurance' in the New Testament and a characteristic encouraged by the apostle Paul.

Many secular writers note the important part that faith plays in resilience, and I think it is fair to say that we can speak about spiritual resilience when we are describing the strength that we may find in God to cope with our struggles. This is the theme for these readings, and my prayer is that you will discover the wealth of encouragement there is in scripture to keep going through adversity and hardship, and be reminded how faith can help us recover from setbacks and disappointments.

TONY HORSFALL

The need for resilience

Remember those earlier days after you had received the light, when you endured in a great conflict full of suffering. Sometimes you were publicly exposed to insult and persecution; at other times you stood side by side with those who were so treated. You suffered along with those in prison and joyfully accepted the confiscation of your property, because you knew that you yourselves had better and lasting possessions. So do not throw away your confidence; it will be richly rewarded. You need to persevere so that when you have done the will of God, you will receive what he has promised.

The epistle to the Hebrews was written to encourage Jewish Christians who were in danger of losing their faith through discouragement and difficulty. In this context the writer says they need to persevere, using the Greek word *hupomone*, which, as we have seen, could be translated as 'resilience'.

Resilience can be defined as the ability to keep going during times of difficulty; to bounce back after disappointment; to recover from hurt or injury; to deal effectively with pressure and stress. When we read the situation surrounding these first believers, it is easy to see why they needed resilience. When we think of our own society, and the pressures we face today, we probably feel the same way. All of us have our own personal struggles and experience our share of suffering. The temptation to quit is real, the desire to give up a constant danger.

Here we are reminded that, to do the will of God and to receive the good of all he has promised us, we must find the strength to keep going. Where does such strength come from? From within ourselves, yes, as we find the determination to carry on. But also from outside ourselves, as we begin to learn how to find our strength in God. It is not his will for us to fail or to give up. His help is always available to us, even in our weakness. We have only to call out to him for help and he will come to our aid.

Lord, you know the pressures I face. Give me strength to persevere even when I feel like quitting.

TONY HORSFALL

Finding strength in God

When David and his men reached Ziklag, they found it destroyed by fire and their wives and sons and daughters taken captive. So David and his men wept aloud until they had no strength left to weep. David's two wives had been captured – Ahinoam of Jezreel and Abigail, the widow of Nabal of Carmel. David was greatly distressed because the men were talking of stoning him; each one was bitter in spirit because of his sons and daughters. But David found strength in the Lord his God.

Is this David's darkest day? Having sought temporary refuge among the Philistines from Saul's murderous threats, David has been forced to return to his desert home in Ziklag. A scene of utter devastation awaits David and his men. The encampment was utterly destroyed and looted, their loved ones taken hostage by Amalekite raiders. Battle-hardened soldiers are reduced to tears. In their grief they turn on David, venting their anger on their leader.

Trauma of any kind has a way of knocking us off our feet, of destabilising the steadiest of people. No doubt David too was initially shaken, but he finds equilibrium again by turning to God. In moments of sudden and unexpected crisis we either turn away from God or turn towards him. David chose the latter and to find his strength in the one who was his rock and his refuge.

I imagine David stepping aside for a period of solitude and there turning to God in heartfelt prayer – venting his feelings honestly, expressing his confusion and rage – and yet working his way through his pain to a place of trust in God. Perhaps he even chose to praise God amid his difficulty. Certainly he would have reminded himself of God's promises and asked for divine guidance. Then, when he had recovered his balance, he was ready to step back into the fray and respond to the situation.

This is a pattern we see often in David's psalms, and one that we can follow for ourselves. It reminds us that there is a spiritual dimension to resilience, and that faith in God is an important resource when it comes to coping with life's demands.

Lord, help me to turn towards you in times of stress.

TONY HORSFALL

Practising self-care

Elijah was afraid and ran for his life. When he came to Beersheba in Judah, he left his servant there, while he himself went a day's journey into the wilderness. He came to a broom bush, sat down under it and prayed that he might die. 'I have had enough, Lord,' he said. 'Take my life; I am no better than my ancestors.' Then he lay down under the bush and fell asleep. All at once an angel touched him and said, 'Get up and eat.' He looked around, and there by his head was some bread baked over hot coals, and a jar of water. He ate and drank and then lay down again.

After his success on Mount Carmel against the prophets of Baal, Elijah is suddenly overcome by a feeling of utter despair. Exhausted from the ordeal and fearing for his life, he hides in the desert and begs God to let him die.

God's way of caring for Elijah is to send an angel to attend to his physical needs. What the prophet most requires at this moment is a good meal, some refreshment and a long rest. This may seem like pretty basic care, yet it is exactly what Elijah needs to recover his strength and the angel's practical ministrations are repeated for good measure (vv. 7–9).

Research has shown that there is a physical dimension to resilience that involves looking after ourselves properly. Regular exercise, sufficient sleep, a healthy diet and drinking enough water are just some of the factors highlighted as being vital aspects in self-care. In the demands of daily life, the pressures of work and church responsibilities, it is easy to be overcommitted and to become exhausted. If we continually give out to others without caring for ourselves, we leave ourselves at the risk of operating out of a deficiency of energy and motivation. Left unchecked, such an imbalance can lead to burnout.

Resilient people practise appropriate self-care, not selfishly for their own comfort, but so they can sustain their service for God and others. Be sure to take care of your body as well as your soul.

Lord, my body is a gift from you. Help me to respect it,
and to care for it wisely.

TONY HORSFALL

Looking after your mind

Therefore, I urge you, brothers and sisters, in view of God's mercy, to offer your bodies as a living sacrifice, holy and pleasing to God – this is your true and proper worship. Do not conform to the pattern of this world, but be transformed by the renewing of your mind. Then you will be able to test and approve what God's will is – his good, pleasing and perfect will.

Paul was always urging his followers to give themselves fully to God, and to live radically different lives to that of the pagan world around them. He longed to see them increasingly transformed into Christlikeness, and at the heart of this struggle he recognised the importance of right thinking.

In speaking of the renewal of the mind, Paul is thinking about making sure our thoughts are in line with God's thoughts, that we adopt a Christian world view, whereby we see things from God's perspective. This is not easy to attain, as we all bring with us patterns of thinking from our old lives. Furthermore, we are constantly bombarded by the world's way of thinking. The media, in its many forms, impacts us daily and seeks to influence our thoughts, values and behaviours. The result is that our minds are often full of unhelpful ideas that work against our growth in Christ.

Resilient people guard their minds. They challenge their own thinking so that negative thought patterns do not rob them of their self-worth and self-confidence. They discipline their minds to take in the word of God through study, scripture memorisation and meditation, allowing their thoughts to be shaped by God's truth. Thus their thinking becomes more robust and they are better prepared to withstand the lies of the devil and any falsity in cultural norms. Further, they have a way of interpreting what happens to them in the light of God's purposes.

In particular, they take hold of the promises of God and bring them to mind whenever they need reassurance. They learn to trust God's word more than their feelings or their circumstances, and to walk by faith and not by sight.

Lord, help me to renew my mind, to sift out any unhelpful thinking and to replace it with your truth.

TONY HORSFALL

Validating your emotions

My tears have been my food day and night, while people say to me all day long, 'Where is your God?' These things I remember as I pour out my soul: how I used to go to the house of God under the protection of the Mighty One, with shouts of joy and praise among the festive throng. Why, my soul, are you downcast? Why so disturbed within me? Put your hope in God, for I will yet praise him, my Saviour and my God.

The writer of this psalm is probably a temple musician exiled either in northern Israel or even Babylon. Separated from all that he loves, he experiences a time of reactive depression, which he bravely acknowledges before God and others in this poignant song.

The ability to identify, own and validate our emotions, and to be open about our feelings, is another characteristic of resilient people. Emotions add colour to our lives, but they can also be troublesome, captivating our souls and, if we are not careful, pushing us to behave unhelpfully. All of us must learn how to take control of our emotions rather than allow them to control us, although that is not the same as suppressing them or pretending we don't have them.

The psalmist is honest about his feelings of depression, which takes real courage, but is not content to wallow in self-pity. Rather, he questions the validity of his downheartedness in the light of what he knows about God, and speaks words of hope to himself. He chooses to be optimistic about the future, believing things will change, and although he continues to battle with his emotions, this faith-filled response sets his feet on solid ground.

Crying is normal in times of loss, and there is nothing to be ashamed of in shedding tears. Tears have a way of bringing healing because they release stress hormones from the body, which is why we feel better after a good cry. Expressing what we are feeling through writing, art or music also helps us to cope, as does talking things through with a good listener.

Lord, you understand how I feel. I have no need to be ashamed.
Help me to trust in you even when I feel all at sea.

TONY HORSFALL

Building a support network

Two are better than one, because they have a good return for their labour: if either of them falls down, one can help the other up. But pity anyone who falls and has no one to help them up. Also, if two lie down together, they will keep warm. But how can one keep warm alone? Though one may be overpowered, two can defend themselves. A cord of three strands is not quickly broken.

The author of Ecclesiastes is usually identified as King Solomon, a man noted for his wisdom. Here he speaks about the importance of nurturing and developing good friendships as a way of coping with the challenges of life.

Among the many benefits of close, supportive relationships, he highlights four valuable outcomes: being able to work together on a task; helping each other recover after falling; lending emotional warmth during chilly times of adversity; and offering mutual protection in times of attack. Who would not appreciate such help? As believers we are not called to be independent, but interdependent, and such quality relationships are a great source of strength when times are hard.

Good friendships require an investment of time and energy, but this proves abundantly worthwhile in the long run, for our best support in life usually comes from those closest to us. Keep in touch with your friends; meet them for coffee or a meal; be open and honest with them. If you have such people around you, don't take them for granted – appreciate them and let them know how important they are to you.

Despite the highly connected world in which we live, many people remain lonely and isolated. If that is how you feel, ask God to give you one or two good friends with whom you can share in this way. Remember that to have friends we must also be a friend. Don't let the fear of rejection prevent you from reaching out to others.

All of us should be ready to welcome others into the circle of our friendship and to keep our eyes open for those who are lonely. Friendship is a God-given way of maintaining our resilience in life.

Lord, thank you for my friendships. Help me to be a good friend to others.

TONY HORSFALL

Seeing the bigger picture

His brothers then came and threw themselves down before him. 'We are your slaves,' they said. But Joseph said to them, 'Don't be afraid. Am I in the place of God? You intended to harm me, but God intended it for good to accomplish what is now being done, the saving of many lives. So then, don't be afraid. I will provide for you and your children.' And he reassured them and spoke kindly to them.

The story of Joseph and his brothers is told in Genesis 37—50 and provides a remarkable example of resilience. Despite his being cruelly betrayed by his siblings, being sold into slavery in Egypt and ending up in prison through false accusation, Joseph is able to forgive his brothers. Not only that, he can also see God's purpose in all that happened, and how God's favour on his life has enabled him to provide for his family during the time of famine.

The ability to make sense of what happens to us in life, and to have a way of interpreting our suffering, greatly enhances resilience. Viktor Frankl, in his famous book *Man's Search for Meaning*, reflects on his time in a German concentration camp. He noticed that the prisoners who coped best were those who could find a sense of meaning even in such tragic surroundings.

Joseph interprets what has happened to him through the lens of faith. He can see a bigger picture. In his providence God has allowed these things to happen to him and has given him a place of prominence in Egypt so that he is able to save his family. This understanding gives his suffering meaning and enables him to rise above the natural temptation to be bitter.

There is a mystery to the providence of God, and it can best be understood with hindsight and the passing of time, but it is comforting to know that, as the apostle Paul said, God is able to bring good even out of the bad things that happen (Romans 8:28). We are not the victims of chance or fate – there is a guiding hand.

Lord, I don't always understand all that happens to me,
but I dare to trust that you are in control.

TONY HORSFALL

What suffering produces

Not only so, but we also glory in our sufferings, because we know that suffering produces perseverance; perseverance, character; and character, hope. And hope does not put us to shame, because God's love has been poured out into our hearts through the Holy Spirit, who has been given to us.

In our risk-averse society, it seems strange to say that we can rejoice or glory in our sufferings. Suffering is something to be avoided at all costs, isn't it? Don't we have the right to a happy, carefree life, and isn't God the guarantor of that? The apostle Paul seems to disagree. Suffering is inevitable in this troubled world, but it is not meaningless or without value. Suffering produces something in us. If we allow it, suffering can change us for the better. It can help us to develop the characteristic of perseverance, the strength to keep going despite setbacks and disappointments.

We noted before that the Greek word translated as 'perseverance' (*hupomone*) is the equivalent of our modern word 'resilience'. Resilience is like a muscle; it is strengthened by having something to push against. When we face adversity, we can either give in and buckle under or choose to fight back and overcome. Every time we choose to fight back, our resilience is strengthened and we develop greater perseverance for the next challenge.

Perseverance itself produces a change in us. When we come through suffering we are often more compassionate, more humble and more dependent on God. Our character has been transformed. At the same time, the Holy Spirit, who enables us to respond to suffering in this way, gives us hope that God's good purpose for us will come to pass. He assures us that nothing can separate us from the love of God (Romans 8:38–39).

We don't ask to suffer, but if suffering comes our way we dare to believe that God can use it for our growth. Suffering can be productive in our lives when we meet it with God's strength. In that we can rejoice.

Lord, thank you that I do not face suffering alone,
but with the help of your Spirit.

TONY HORSFALL

Firm to the end

When word came to Sanballat, Tobiah, Geshem the Arab and the rest of our enemies that I had rebuilt the wall and not a gap was left in it – though up to that time I had not set the doors in the gates – Sanballat and Geshem sent me this message: 'Come, let us meet together in one of the villages on the plain of Ono.' But they were scheming to harm me; so I sent messengers to them with this reply: 'I am carrying on a great project and cannot go down. Why should the work stop while I leave it and go down to you?' Four times they sent me the same message, and each time I gave them the same answer.

Nehemiah is a wonderful example of steadfastness, of persevering through difficulty. He was called by God to rebuild the walls of Jerusalem during the return from exile. His great achievement is that he took a group of dispirited individuals and inspired them to work together, so that despite much fierce opposition they were able to complete the task in just 52 days (Nehemiah 6:15–16).

The story of the rebuilding is recorded in Nehemiah 1—6. It feels like a boxing match in which Nehemiah is on the ropes conceding blow after blow, yet standing his ground. The opposition comes from powerful individuals, like Sanballat, Tobiah and Geshem, who do not want the Jews to succeed and do all they can to undermine their plans. They taunt and ridicule them, stirring up trouble and intimidating the workers. When all this fails, they attack Nehemiah personally, slandering him and threatening him with violence.

How does Nehemiah stand firm in the face of such opposition? He knows that God is with him and has called him to do the work. This sense of vocation is a powerful factor in his resilience. He knows that what he is doing is worthwhile, that it matters to God and God's people. This is why he calls it a 'great project'. He must remain faithful to the task because it has been given him by God. This strengthens his resolve and enables him to stand his ground. He refuses to step down.

Lord, strengthen my own resolve to serve you without giving up.

TONY HORSFALL

God's surpassing power

But we have this treasure in jars of clay to show that this all-surpassing power is from God and not from us. We are hard pressed on every side, but not crushed; perplexed, but not in despair; persecuted, but not abandoned; struck down, but not destroyed. We always carry around in our body the death of Jesus, so that the life of Jesus may also be revealed in our body.

If anyone deserves the description of resilient it is the apostle Paul. He suffered so much as he sought to share the good news of Jesus throughout the Mediterranean world. Shipwrecks, beatings and imprisonments were his lot, as well as much hard work, many sleepless nights, relentless opposition and constant danger.

Paul was no superhero, however, but an ordinary man aware of his weakness and limitations. The 'treasure' of the gospel, he reminds us, is contained in jars of clay. Just as merchants would store their grain or commodities in plain, earthenware jars, so God has put his wonderful salvation message in the hands of human beings, who are weak, frail and fallible. It seems that God has taken a great risk in doing so, but that is how he chooses to work.

We are not left alone in our weakness, however, because God's power is available to us. That power is able to help us overcome the challenges we face – it surpasses the downwards pull of our inadequacy and enables us to do more than we think we can. When people observe our lives, they can only draw one conclusion: God must be at work in this person's life.

Resilience is a form of resurrection. Paul's experience of suffering enables the life of God to be expressed through him to the blessing of others. His suffering is a way of sharing in the death of Jesus and the effectiveness of his ministry a way of sharing in his resurrection power.

We may not be called to suffer as much as Paul did, but the same all-surpassing power of God is available to us as we face our own struggles.

Lord, sometimes I am so conscious of my weakness. Thank you that your all-surpassing power is at work in me today.

TONY HORSFALL

Grace that is sufficient

Therefore, in order to keep me from becoming conceited, I was given a thorn in my flesh, a messenger of Satan, to torment me. Three times I pleaded with the Lord to take it away from me. But he said to me, 'My grace is sufficient for you, for my power is made perfect in weakness.' Therefore I will boast all the more gladly about my weaknesses, so that Christ's power may rest on me. That is why, for Christ's sake, I delight in weaknesses, in insults, in hardships, in persecutions, in difficulties. For when I am weak, then I am strong.

Not only did Paul suffer because of the ministry God had given him, but he also suffered because of a severe affliction, described here as a thorn in his flesh. We do not know exactly to what he is referring, except that it appears to have been something physical, extremely painful and chronic. Satan was using it to torment Paul, and he wanted to be rid of it.

Paul was an experienced prayer warrior who had seen many answers to his prayers, but all his attempts to find deliverance were unsuccessful. He was left battered and baffled. Then, at the moment of absolute weakness, God spoke a personal word to reassure him: 'My grace is sufficient for you, for my power is made perfect in weakness' (v. 9). These words completely changed his attitude towards his suffering.

Grace in this context refers to God's unlimited strength freely made available to us in our need. God does not always choose to deliver us from our pain but he does promise to give sufficient grace so we can bear it, and do so with a positive attitude. His promise is that his power will rest on us in our weakness, giving us the strength we need to endure. So gentle is this ministry of the Spirit that we may not even be aware of it ourselves, but somehow we pull through. And this God-given strength is sufficient for any and every circumstance.

Paul learned from this not to be ashamed of his weakness, but to rejoice in it because God could still be glorified in his life.

Lord, today I believe your grace is sufficient for me.

TONY HORSFALL

The helper

'If you love me, keep my commands. And I will ask the Father, and he will give you another advocate to help you and be with you for ever – the Spirit of truth. The world cannot accept him, because it neither sees him nor knows him. But you know him, for he lives with you and will be in you. I will not leave you as orphans; I will come to you.'

Shortly before his death, Jesus gathered his disciples together to share with them the passover meal and to prepare them for his departure. He was conscious that they would feel grief when he was no longer with them, that the task ahead of them would be challenging and that they would face great opposition. His intention, therefore, in the discourse recorded in John 13—17 is to encourage and strengthen them – to increase their resilience.

The disciples had been living closely with Jesus for three years and his death would leave them bereft. Indeed, Jesus says they will feel orphaned, such will be the impact of his death upon them. His promise to them is that he will not leave them alone. He will not abandon them, but will send the Holy Spirit to be their helper.

The word translated here as 'advocate' is also translated as 'helper', 'comforter' and 'counsellor'. Each word is a way of describing the fortifying work of the Spirit in our lives. The Greek word is *paraclete*, and it means 'one who draws alongside'. The picture is of someone who comes to our aid when we are in distress.

Imagine your vehicle has broken down at the side of the motorway. You are in danger because of the speed of the traffic and are helpless to repair the vehicle, so you call for assistance from a breakdown recovery service. Soon an expert is on hand to reassure you, make the necessary repairs and send you happily on your way. How relieved you are!

This is like the work of the Spirit on our behalf. We are never left to face difficulties by ourselves. Jesus has sent the Spirit to be with us and day by day he is available to draw alongside and strengthen us.

Lord, today you are my helper.

TONY HORSFALL

Jesus, our example

Therefore, since we are surrounded by such a great cloud of witnesses, let us throw off everything that hinders and the sin that so easily entangles. And let us run with perseverance the race marked out for us, fixing our eyes on Jesus, the pioneer and perfecter of faith. For the joy that was set before him he endured the cross, scorning its shame, and sat down at the right hand of the throne of God. Consider him who endured such opposition from sinners, so that you will not grow weary and lose heart.

The book of Hebrews was written to encourage believers who were in danger of giving up their faith. After giving a long list of notable examples of endurance from the Old Testament in chapter 11 (the cloud of witnesses), the writer then turns to the supreme example of resilience – Jesus. The way he persevered when facing the cross is an inspiration to all who follow him to remain steadfast.

Jesus endured the cross and all the physical pain associated with such a cruel and agonising death. He felt the agony of it in every part of his being, yet did not shrink back. Likewise, he experienced the psychological pain of it – the shame of being publicly stripped, the cruel mockery of the soldiers and the vindictive abuse of the passers-by – but did not flinch.

He was able to do this because he was strengthened by the joy set before him: the prospect of seeing a multitude of people reconciled to God by his death, and living in relationship with God as their Father (see Revelation 7:9). This hope kept him going, and the knowledge that he sacrificed himself so that we might be among that multitude can fortify us as we seek to follow him today.

How can we fix our eyes on Jesus? We are to look away from our sorrows and difficulties and look instead towards Jesus. As we consider again all that he has done for us, and the love he showed for us at Calvary, we too can find renewed strength and purpose to carry on.

Lord, fill my heart afresh with love for Jesus so that I do not lose heart.

TONY HORSFALL

Our great high priest

Therefore, since we have a great high priest who has ascended into heaven, Jesus the Son of God, let us hold firmly to the faith we profess. For we do not have a high priest who is unable to feel sympathy for our weaknesses, but we have one who has been tempted in every way, just as we are – yet he did not sin. Let us then approach God's throne of grace with confidence, so that we may receive mercy and find grace to help us in our time of need.

Here is another reason to endure – Jesus is our merciful and faithful high priest. Having lived our life, and died in our place, he rose again and is now seated at the right hand of the Father in heaven, where he constantly prays for us (Hebrews 7:25). This is not a factor that secular research into resilience will ever recognise, but it is a powerful encouragement to those of us who believe in Christ.

Jesus understands what it is to be human. Not only did he experience the suffering of the cross, but during his earthly life he felt all the things that we feel. He knew rejection, disappointment, betrayal, grief and fierce opposition. He was tempted by the devil and let down by his closest friends. Yet he did not give up.

This means that when we come to him in prayer, asking for his strength to continue, he meets us with a merciful response. He is compassionate and understanding of our weakness, failures and uncertainties. He does not turn us away in disapproval but welcomes us with sympathy and acceptance. More than that, at such moments of great need he pours his grace into our lives, giving us the strength to carry on and sustaining us in the ups and downs of our journey of discipleship. Suffering and hardship can actually bring us closer to him once we realise this dynamic, since we are not afraid to draw near. We know we can approach his throne just as we are.

Remember that today Jesus is aware of you and your circumstances. Be assured he is ready, willing and able to help you.

Lord, I turn to you for help, knowing you will never turn away.

TONY HORSFALL

Titus and Philemon:
a gift of encouragement

Over the next fortnight we will digest the letters to Titus and Philemon, which complete the large Pauline section of the New Testament. They are very different. Scholars see the latter as pure Paul without a doubt, but note signs of editing in the former common to the other pastoral letters of 1 and 2 Timothy. These letters address discipline and doctrine and speak into a later stage of church development than Paul's early writings.

The letter to Titus speaks of the given-ness of Christianity in the revelation of God in Jesus Christ, in whom the grace of God has appeared (Titus 2:11). Accepting and handing on that revelation is pivotal and brings with it the anointing of the Holy Spirit. Titus contains an appeal to welcome and imitate God's pure love revealed in Jesus Christ and to abandon all that distracts from this. In our study we engage with references to grace and the Holy Spirit with an invitation to ponder and open ourselves afresh to God's gift of himself to us.

In contrast to Titus, with its wide-ranging pastoral and teaching brief, Philemon is short and focused. It was written by Paul to Philemon on behalf of Philemon's runaway slave Onesimus, bidding his owner forgive him and offering to clear the slave's debt. While the letter's context makes for strange reading, it is wrong to see it as commending slavery. Rather its emphasis is upon the transformation of the slave Onesimus by the good news of Jesus Christ, making him 'more than a slave, a beloved brother' (Philemon 16, NRSV) to Philemon his master. We engage with the paradox of how the quest to build God's inclusive kingdom in the world continues through time – nowadays countering slavery – yet the distinctive inclusion of Christianity lies in God's invitation to welcome eternal life.

Also over the next two weeks, we will pause to reflect on readings for the birthday of St John the Baptist and the Feast of St Peter and St Paul, which add spice to the spiritual nourishment provided by Paul's letters. Both epistles bring wisdom about the Spirit-given ministry of encouragement.

JOHN TWISLETON

Gifts of encouragement

Paul, a servant of God and an apostle of Jesus Christ, for the sake of the faith of God's elect and the knowledge of the truth that is in accordance with godliness, in the hope of eternal life that God, who never lies, promised before the ages began – in due time he revealed his word through the proclamation with which I have been entrusted by the command of God our Saviour, To Titus, my loyal child in the faith we share: Grace and peace from God the Father and Christ Jesus our Saviour.

We all need people to look up to. I think back on people who had something about them I couldn't explain, but their occasional words to me had a force that countered my selfish agenda. They were people who generally treated me as better than I am and pointed me to a brighter place, and in the process they brought the best out of me. Sometimes we recognise ourselves in a similar role towards others, exercising a gift of encouragement.

Titus looked up to Paul as a spiritual father, evident from the initial greeting in this letter, which is also an imparting of wisdom to Titus as church leader. The earlier writings of Paul to Corinth, Rome and Thessalonica speak of faith as one-to-one communion with God. The later letters, like Titus, possibly edited after Paul's death, encourage the corporate faith of the church, 'the faith of God's elect and the knowledge of the truth that is in accordance with godliness' (v. 1).

Building such faith, the basis of Christian unity, is Paul's passion as 'a servant of God and apostle of Jesus Christ' (v. 1). Through reflection on scripture and fellowship with others in the good news of Christ, we build that passion. The gift of encouragement flows from such a passion, though it is inseparable from human sympathy, so our passage speaks of faith and truth being linked to godliness and the gifts of grace and peace.

Look back thankfully on the grace of God you have received from others. Pray that grace will be more evident in your life, so as to bring those in your circle closer to Christ and his people.

JOHN TWISLETON

Godly church oversight

Appoint elders in every town, as I directed you: someone who is blameless, married only once, whose children are believers, not accused of debauchery and not rebellious. For a bishop, as God's steward, must be blameless; he must not be arrogant or quick-tempered or addicted to wine or violent or greedy for gain; but he must be hospitable, a lover of goodness, prudent, upright, devout, and self-controlled. He must have a firm grasp of the word that is trustworthy in accordance with the teaching, so that he may be able both to preach with sound doctrine and to refute those who contradict it.

Leadership in Christianity exists at many levels. If my parents hadn't led by example in showing Christianity as something vital to life, I probably wouldn't be writing this! Being a good mum or dad is as important as being a good pastor. Passages on the task and qualities of overseers or bishops should be read in the context of the call to holiness of every Christian, for without holiness we're unlikely to have a good influence upon our circle.

If that circle is the whole body of Christ, then seeking holiness is all the more important. The pastoral letters make a 'big ask' of church leaders, in contrast to the mercy shown to human failings in church members elsewhere in the New Testament. The bishop or overseer has the perilous task 'both to preach with sound doctrine and to refute those who contradict it' (v. 9). Churches don't grow without such teaching, which alone has the power to transform people. If the teacher fails personally, his or her teaching falls on deaf ears.

As Paul explains in Romans 1:16, the gospel is 'the power of God for salvation to everyone who has faith'. However much care leaders give, it will fall short without the call to repent and believe that opens God's people again and again to God. Such submission by church members, including church leaders, to God's word helps keep the Spirit's anointing upon the church.

'Respect those who labour among you, and have charge of you in the Lord and admonish you; esteem them very highly in love because of their work' (1 Thessalonians 5:12–13).

JOHN TWISLETON

Seeking God's pure love

To the pure all things are pure, but to the corrupt and unbelieving nothing is pure. Their very minds and consciences are corrupted. They profess to know God, but they deny him by their actions. They are detestable, disobedient, unfit for any good work. But as for you, teach what is consistent with sound doctrine.

I remember a saintly bishop issuing a warning at a time of church conflict along the lines of 'It's less important to be high church, middle church or low church as to be deep church.' If more decisions in the world were made by holy people, can we doubt that the world would be a better place? When we read 'to the pure all things are pure' (v. 15), it's a reminder that when we seek and find the indwelling of the Holy Spirit, our vision isn't distracted by peripheral issues but looks to affirm and strengthen what's good, truthful and beautiful, wherever we see it.

The sense of these verses, though, is in no way indifferent to faithfulness to specific truth. The pastoral epistles address divisions that occurred early on in the church linked to both shallow discipleship and deviation from the truth of God revealed in Jesus Christ. The description of Christian people who 'profess to know God, but... deny him by their actions' is close to home. How many of us live with the self-surrender God calls us to? By contrast Paul's appeal that Titus 'teach what is consistent with sound doctrine' is a challenge, especially for church leaders.

That both 'minds and consciences are corrupted' by wrong belief is evident to the writer as it should be evident to us. Wrongdoing comes partly from wrong believing. At the heart of this letter there's an appeal to welcome and imitate God's pure love revealed in Jesus Christ. The anguish within the letter is about people and issues distracting from this core truth of salvation.

Reflect on this passage, centring on the purity, love and truth that are found in Jesus Christ, mindful of his words: 'You will know the truth, and the truth will make you free' (John 8:32).

JOHN TWISLETON

The grace of God has appeared

For the grace of God has appeared, bringing salvation to all, training us to renounce impiety and worldly passions, and in the present age to live lives that are self-controlled, upright, and godly, while we wait for the blessed hope and the manifestation of the glory of our great God and Saviour, Jesus Christ. He it is who gave himself for us that he might redeem us from all iniquity and purify for himself a people of his own who are zealous for good deeds.

'The grace of God has appeared' (v. 11). In six words we have a summary of Christianity. God, seen up to the time of Christ as above and beyond this world, has become part of it! Few passages capture so succinctly the 'given-ness' of Christianity as something from God with spiritual and moral force.

This 'given-ness' lies in a historical revelation, timed by God in his wisdom – a history subject to our examination, calling forth a personal response, since 'he it is who gave himself for us that he might redeem us from all iniquity and purify for himself a people of his own who are zealous for good deeds' (v. 14).

What does it mean to be 'zealous for good deeds'? It is not to be like the apocryphal lady who spent her life on others – and you could tell the 'others' by their hunted look! We need zeal, and we get it from contemplating Christ, as well as from sympathy. The overflow of that prayer should be unforced since prayer pushes our selfish concerns away and opens our eyes to what good God needs us to do around us. John Wesley's advice was: 'Do all the good you can, by all the means you can, in all the ways you can, in all the places you can, at all the times you can, to all the people you can, as long as ever you can.'

God's grace has appeared in Jesus Christ, and that help is ever with us. As we seek the Lord day by day, we lose self-focus so as to do good deeds as instruments of his outgoing love.

May the grace of God appear in and through us today.

JOHN TWISLETON

Submission

Remind them to be subject to rulers and authorities, to be obedient, to be ready for every good work, to speak evil of no one, to avoid quarrelling, to be gentle, and to show every courtesy to everyone.

Over my years in ministry I've regularly encouraged assertiveness among believers vis-à-vis the authorities. I recall training priests among indigenous people in Guyana with regard to some of the difficulties they experienced with gold miners who polluted the rivers, a problem that remains ongoing. Finding courage to speak truth to power is difficult, but it's essential at times, especially when it's clear there's serious injustice afoot.

While the Holy Spirit at times works through our assertive action to shake society into being a better place, he also gifts his people with self-control 'to be subject to rulers and authorities' (v. 1), since failure to respect the laws and norms of society threatens the common good and undermines individual freedom. To be obedient is an unfashionable virtue, yet it shines out from the life of Christ who was 'obedient to the point of death' (Philippians 2:8). Obedience to those in authority is nothing servile for Christians. It is about the best harnessing of our energies 'for every good work'.

I remember during my time in Guyana being given shocking counsel by a wise Pentecostal pastor that built from this passage: 'You can't be right with God unless you're right with those who are over you in the Lord'. Being 'right' with civic or church leaders doesn't exclude respectful disagreement, recognises their need to answer to God but calls in the end for submission to them. The wider aspirations in verse 2 are pivotal to any Christian community: 'to speak evil of no one, to avoid quarrelling, to be gentle, and to show every courtesy to everyone'. Such qualities demonstrate a readiness to give people the benefit of the doubt that flows from a conviction that God in his great mercy gives us individually such a benefit.

'May God grant to the living grace, to the departed rest, to the church and the world peace and concord, and to us sinners eternal life'
(prayer on the west wall of Westminster Abbey).

JOHN TWISLETON

Farewell to old ways

For we ourselves were once foolish, disobedient, led astray, slaves to various passions and pleasures, passing our days in malice and envy, despicable, hating one another. But when the goodness and loving-kindness of God our Saviour appeared, he saved us, not because of any works of righteousness that we had done, but according to his mercy, through the water of rebirth and renewal by the Holy Spirit.

'Are you saved?' When asked this question, I say, 'I've been saved, I'm being saved and I will be saved,' and I point to this passage, which reminds us of baptism's significance in an ongoing process. As one who entered 'the water of rebirth and renewal' (v. 5) myself as an infant, personal faith has followed my baptism. Nowadays it's often the other way around. It was for Paul, whose entry into the Christian church was so dramatic. He can well speak of once having been 'foolish, disobedient, led astray' (v. 3) and of once being reliant on 'works of righteousness' (v. 5) rather than God's free grace.

Scholars see in this passage a development from Paul's earliest writings, which stress faith more than baptism as essential to salvation. Paul's faith came in a flash on Damascus Road, after which he joined the church through Ananias (Acts 9:10–19). Passing through the water of baptism brings church membership. It comes with the obligation to put that baptism into practice by drowning sinful passions and welcoming the refreshment of the Holy Spirit in an ongoing way – a process we call salvation.

This passage links to Christ's statement about being born again 'of water and Spirit' (John 3:5), that is, baptism and faith. Both scriptures give us cause to ponder God's gift to us and to open ourselves afresh to his transforming work. Opening ourselves to the Spirit is also encouraged by the coming-to-faith stories of church members we encounter throughout our Christian life.

Reflect on the new life that is yours through 'the water of rebirth and renewal by the Holy Spirit'. What does it mean for you to be 'saved'? You could prepare a short testimony for use when people ask you about the reality of your faith.

JOHN TWISLETON

Seeking the Holy Spirit

This Spirit he poured out on us richly through Jesus Christ our Saviour, so that, having been justified by his grace, we might become heirs according to the hope of eternal life. The saying is sure.

Some years back I experienced a crisis of faith. God seemed a long way off. I went to talk to a Mirfield monk, who gave me this advice: 'Maybe it's not God that's gone but your vision of him. Seek from the Holy Spirit a vision more to God's dimensions and less to your own.' I did seek and I did experience the 'Spirit poured out on [me] richly through Jesus Christ [my] Saviour' (v. 6). Those personal pronouns are a reminder that Bible verses can come alive in our experience.

One of the biggest brains in the church, the 13th-century priest Thomas Aquinas, was responsible for systematising thinking about God. Having completed his *Summa Theologica*, he said that it was all useless as straw without a living experience of God. Thomas taught that the Holy Spirit is always willing to come to us, even if there are special occasions, such as baptism, that are seen as his unique work and gift, as we saw yesterday.

When we call on the Spirit to refresh our flagging faith, we call on the whole of God, especially the work of Jesus Christ our Saviour. Easter and Pentecost are inseparable – the Father sends his Son to die and rise so that the Holy Spirit can be poured out. That we are 'justified by his grace' – put into right relation with God – links to both the historical work of Christ and our calling here and now, for the gift of the Spirit who makes us 'heirs according to the hope of eternal life' (v. 7).

How do you see the Holy Spirit? As the shadowy 'Holy Ghost', as in former language, or as a living reality who impacts your life through word, sacrament and prayer building up the assurance and hope spoken of in this passage?

'Come, Thou Holy Spirit, come – bend the stubborn heart and will;
melt the frozen, warm the chill; guide the steps that go astray'
(Hymns Ancient and Modern Revised, Number 156).

JOHN TWISLETON

Avoid stupid controversies

I desire that you insist on these things, so that those who have come to believe in God may be careful to devote themselves to good works; these things are excellent and profitable to everyone. But avoid stupid controversies, genealogies, dissensions, and quarrels about the law, for they are unprofitable and worthless. After a first and second admonition, have nothing more to do with anyone who causes divisions, since you know that such a person is perverted and sinful, being self-condemned.

Once I celebrated Easter twice, through catching spring sunshine on holiday in Greece. I wondered how the founder of Christianity, whose last words to his followers were 'that they may all be one' (John 17:22), would see this dual celebration? Those words, echoed in the pastoral epistles, show Christian divisions were lamented from the very start.

The earliest letters of the apostle Paul thrill with the immediacy of the risen Lord Jesus and the imminence of his return to gather his followers to glory, with little concern for church order. In this concluding section of the letter to Titus, we see in contrast a developing concern about structuring the church on right doctrine, discipline and oversight.

That Orthodox, Protestant and Catholic Christians follow different church calendars is sad – a legacy of controversies that may indeed be labelled 'unprofitable', let alone 'worthless' or even 'stupid'. The public perception of Christians is damaged by disunity. However, much spiritual unity is growing across traditions – I think of how the Orthodox 'Jesus Prayer' is widely used nowadays in the western church.

Titus concludes with counsel for a church leader on countering hypocrisy and division in the Christian community, with dissenters given but two chances to toe the line. Such severity reflects the gravity of disunity. It challenges Christians today to affirm all that they have in common and to be alert to tendencies that run counter to mainstream belief and practice.

Is there a local church you've never visited? Why not go to one of their services to get a feel for that Christian community and build a personal link with them?

JOHN TWISLETON

Nativity of St John the Baptist

And you, child, will be called the prophet of the Most High; for you will go before the Lord to prepare his ways, to give knowledge of salvation to his people by the forgiveness of their sins. By the tender mercy of our God, the dawn from on high will break upon us, to give light to those who sit in darkness and in the shadow of death.

Our cycle of Pauline readings pauses today to mark the holy day of the Nativity of St John the Baptist. The prophecy spoken by John's father Zechariah at his birth, known as the Benedictus, is used in churches day by day at morning prayer on account of its dawn reference. John's birth, heralding that of Christ his cousin, is 'by the tender mercy of our God', who daily brings 'the dawn from on high [to] break upon us' (v. 78).

If John's birth was the dawn heralding the coming of Christ our light, Christians might be seen as beacons shining with his light to serve 'those who sit in darkness and in the shadow of death' (v. 79). God's love like the sun comes 'new every morning' (Lamentations 3:23), but we need to make time to welcome its kindling day by day. Some years back, I learned to start the day with a morning offering: after putting my feet on the floor, but before I stand up out of bed, I say, 'Lord, I thank you for your love for me and for all, and welcome that love afresh. Take and use me to your praise and service.' It's a good first act of the day.

This special day in the church calendar is an opportunity to rekindle the light of the Lord in our lives by heeding John's invitation to behold the Lamb of God (see John 1:29) and imitating his determination to counter self-interest, as expressed in his words: '[Christ] must increase, but I must decrease' (John 3:30).

Lord Jesus, on this feast of St John the Baptist,
may your light scatter any darkness within me,
rekindle my love for you and make me your beacon. Amen

JOHN TWISLETON

Outgoing love

When I remember you in my prayers, I always thank my God because I hear of your love for all the saints and your faith toward the Lord Jesus. I pray that the sharing of your faith may become effective when you perceive all the good that we may do for Christ. I have indeed received much joy and encouragement from your love, because the hearts of the saints have been refreshed through you, my brother.

'Two men looked through prison bars. One saw mud and one saw stars.' The letter to Philemon illustrates the outgoing focus we gain in Jesus Christ, which defies self-pity. As a letter from prison, it's a vivid demonstration of how the Holy Spirit grants Christians outgoing love even when they're in dark places. Looking through the bars of his own prison, the apostle Paul sees stars – in this case the opportunity to write a letter aimed at reconciling Christians for the greater good of the Lord's work.

In the New Testament, the letter to Philemon sits between two other epistles traditionally viewed as being written by Paul – Titus and Hebrews. But while the authorship of these two letters, especially the latter, is disputed, there's no question among scholars that the apostle wrote Philemon. It's his shortest letter, and, although it is directed to his fellow church leader in Colossae, it lacks the wide-ranging pastoral and teaching brief of the letter to Titus. The letter is focused: it addresses Philemon on behalf of his runaway slave Onesimus, commends him to his owner, bids him forgive the man and offers to clear his debt.

In the letter's opening paragraph, Paul relays to Philemon feedback that he has gleaned from their fellows – that through the bishop (Philemon's likely office) 'the hearts of the saints have been refreshed'. Such a gift of encouragement lends Paul confidence to make his request for Onesimus. Unlike Titus, this is no apostle-to-apostle missionary letter, but one that touches on and appeals for basic Christian generosity.

Lord, you kept Paul outwardly focused in his troubles.
Lift our eyes from our problems so we can see your invitations.

JOHN TWISLETON

Usefulness to God

For this reason, though I am bold enough in Christ to command you to do your duty, yet I would rather appeal to you on the basis of love – and I, Paul, do this as an old man, and now also as a prisoner of Christ Jesus. I am appealing to you for my child, Onesimus, whose father I have become during my imprisonment. Formerly he was useless to you, but now he is indeed useful both to you and to me. I am sending him, that is, my own heart, back to you. I wanted to keep him with me, so that he might be of service to me in your place during my imprisonment for the gospel; but I preferred to do nothing without your consent, in order that your good deed might be voluntary and not something forced.

There is a wordplay in this passage on the convert slave's name Onesimus, which means 'useful'. On the subject of conversion, Paul writes elsewhere how God has 'rescued us from the power of darkness and transferred us into the kingdom of his beloved Son' (Colossians 1:13). Useless groping in darkness and futility gives way in Christ to a new sense of purpose and usefulness under God. Such sentiment lies behind Paul's play on words: 'Formerly he was useless to you, but now he is indeed useful both to you and to me' (v. 11) – to which one might add 'and to God'.

How much love do we invest in our circle? How is it allied to prayer for friends to realise more fully their usefulness to God? Sometimes the gift of discernment comes our way, so when we have a friend's open ear we are moved to make a suggestion that might draw their gifts further into God's praise and service. Paul's request flows from a deep love for Onesimus, described as his own heart, and his appeal to Philemon is stated to be on the basis of love.

In your love, Lord, inspire in us wise choices and words,
so we can be most useful to you and to those in our circle. Amen

JOHN TWISLETON

Divine inclusion

Perhaps this is the reason he was separated from you for a while, so that you might have him back for ever, no longer as a slave but more than a slave, a beloved brother – especially to me but how much more to you, both in the flesh and in the Lord. So if you consider me your partner, welcome him as you would welcome me. If he has wronged you in any way, or owes you anything, charge that to my account. I, Paul, am writing this with my own hand: I will repay it. I say nothing about your owing me even your own self. Yes, brother, let me have this benefit from you in the Lord! Refresh my heart in Christ.

The letter to Philemon today sits uncomfortably in a world that is still challenging slavery. But the emphasis in the letter lies upon the wondrous transformation of the slave Onesimus, of his master Philemon and of Paul himself into the unending fellowship of Christ. Paul writes elsewhere that 'in Christ Jesus you are all children of God through faith… there is no longer slave or free… all of you are one in Christ Jesus' (Galatians 3:26, 28).

Through his conversion, Onesimus is 'more than a slave, a beloved brother' (v. 16) to Philemon, his master, Paul writes. His separation, though apparently linked to Onesimus' misdemeanour, is said to have been 'for a while, so that you might have him back for ever' (v. 15). Though the church's quest to establish God's kingdom in the world works out through time, such as in challenging the institution of slavery, its ultimate sights are on including forever as many as can be included among those belonging to God as King. 'This is eternal life, that [we] may know… the only true God, and Jesus Christ whom [he has] sent' (John 17:3).

The ongoing question of tackling slavery is beyond this short reflection. That a slave and a slave owner from long ago remain included in a life beyond this world is something awesome, as is the opening of any heart to Jesus Christ as Lord.

Look back on occasions when you heard of someone's life changed through Christ's agency, and allow the Holy Spirit to warm your heart through that memory.

JOHN TWISLETON

True encouragement

Confident of your obedience, I am writing to you, knowing that you will do even more than I say. One thing more – prepare a guest room for me, for I am hoping through your prayers to be restored to you. Epaphras, my fellow-prisoner in Christ Jesus, sends greetings to you, and so do Mark, Aristarchus, Demas, and Luke, my fellow-workers. The grace of the Lord Jesus Christ be with your spirit.

Paul's letter to Philemon ends on an encouraging note with greetings from his fellow workers, including Epaphras, his fellow prisoner. The apostle states his confidence that Philemon will do even more than he says. Philemon, Paul implies, will do more than forgive Onesimus. He might seize the opportunity to welcome the presumed bearer of the letter into Christian mission partnership. That would continue to include Paul, who is himself hoping through Philemon's prayers to be restored to him – a guest room is to be prepared in faith for his release from prison (v. 22).

Paul concludes, 'The grace of the Lord Jesus Christ be with your spirit' (v. 25) – speaking to us as it did to Philemon of the wonder of God's capacity to treat us honourably despite our failings, and his invitation for us to treat others in similar fashion, just as the apostle treated the runaway slave Onesimus graciously and not as he deserved.

Behind this story lies one relevant to our lives here and now: the story of one who values less what we have been and more what we can be by the help of the Holy Spirit. True encouragement is in the gift of the same Spirit who, as Spirit of truth, continually helps us see what's wrong in our life. With our ongoing agreement to that – repentance – comes the promise of fresh enfolding in God's love 'poured into our hearts through the Holy Spirit that has been given to us' (Romans 5:5).

Lord, you value less what we have been and more what we can be.
Help us attain the best future as we repent of our failings,
put our faith in you and receive a fresh anointing from the Holy Spirit.

JOHN TWISLETON

Feast of St Peter and St Paul

As for me, I am already being poured out as a libation, and the time of my departure has come. I have fought the good fight, I have finished the race, I have kept the faith. From now on there is reserved for me the crown of righteousness, which the Lord, the righteous judge, will give to me on that day, and not only to me but also to all who have longed for his appearing.

Our completion of the last two Pauline letters in the New Testament coincides with the feast day that Paul shares with Peter, recognising their status as the two pillars of the Christian church. Peter was set apart by Christ with the promise, 'You are Peter, and on this rock I will build my church' (Matthew 16:18), while Paul was set apart by the risen Christ on the road to Damascus. In Paul's words, 'God, who… called me through his grace, was pleased to reveal his Son to me, so that I might proclaim him among the Gentiles' (Galatians 1:15–16).

The passage from 2 Timothy for reading at the Eucharist today captures Paul's yearning for Christ as his joy and prize, which fuelled his energetic ministry of proclamation. 'The time of my departure has come. I have fought the good fight, I have finished the race, I have kept the faith' (vv. 6–7). As one who has longed for Christ's appearing, Paul expects the fulfilment of that longing through death or at Christ's return.

If Paul, with Peter, is a pillar of the church, his teaching grounds us in the sure foundation that lies in Jesus Christ. As we soak in the words of Paul, we gain inner refreshment from one who is the supreme pointer to the risen Lord Jesus. One of the most forward-looking writers in the Bible, Paul thrills us with the future implications of Christ for the universe and our own part as believers in that future, an immortal destiny.

'Not what thou art, nor what thou hast been, beholdeth God
with his merciful eyes, but what thou wouldst be'
(The Cloud of Unknowing, chapter 75).

JOHN TWISLETON

Jeremiah

The book of Jeremiah is a complex work; it is prophetic, but is difficult to date with any degree of precision. The introduction identifies Jeremiah as the central figure of the book and begins by describing both his prophetic call and his reluctance to accept it. The vision accompanying this call suggests some kind of hostile threat coming from the north, but at this point the enemy is not clearly identified. Most of the prophecies that follow declare God's judgement on Judah and Jerusalem, with detailed reasons given as to why that judgement has come about. It was Jeremiah's unenviable task to announce God's judgement to his own people, causing much personal pain and suffering as the people turn against him.

Although most of these early prophecies are difficult to date, as the book progresses the focus does become somewhat clearer. Towards the end of the narrative Judah's enemy is identified as Babylon, a nation that God is using to inflict judgement on Judah and Jerusalem. A number of themes recur, including Judah's apostasy and the stubbornness of the people and their unwillingness to accept correction. Powerful images are employed, such as the depiction of the people as an unfaithful bride, an image also used to great effect elsewhere in the Old Testament (Hosea 1:1—2:1). The persistent reality of chronic lying by the people runs through every aspect of their lives like a poisonous thread.

Time and again Jeremiah calls on the people, urging them to repent and turn away from their evil ways. But their wrongdoing is deep-set and not to be rooted out that easily. As the oracles continue, the sounds of lament become increasingly prevalent – for the people, from the Lord and from Jeremiah himself. The book ends with a flurry of divine retaliation against Babylon for all the indignities the inhabitants of Judah and Jerusalem have suffered at their captors' hands. There are no neat and tidy endings to this book, but our reflections conclude with a piece that is to be found in the midst of these promises of retaliation. It is a piece that proclaims and celebrates the sheer power, wisdom and awesomeness of God, 'the one who formed all things' (Jeremiah 51:19, NRSV).

BARBARA MOSSE

Do not be afraid

Now the word of the Lord came to me saying, 'Before I formed you in the womb I knew you, and before you were born I consecrated you; I appointed you a prophet to the nations.' Then I said, 'Ah, Lord God! Truly I do not know how to speak, for I am only a boy.' But the Lord said to me, 'Do not say, "I am only a boy"; for you shall go to all to whom I send you, and you shall speak whatever I command you. Do not be afraid of them, for I am with you to deliver you, says the Lord. Then the Lord put out his hand and touched my mouth; and the Lord said to me, 'Now I have put my words in your mouth. See, today I appoint you over nations and over kingdoms, to pluck up and to pull down, to destroy and to overthrow, to build and to plant.'

I wonder if you, like me, feel a twinge of sympathetic recognition as you read this passage. The 'Here am I; send him' reaction seems to be a characteristic of humanity throughout the centuries. Jeremiah is certainly not alone here: other Old Testament figures, such as Moses (Exodus 3—4) and Gideon (Judges 6:15), also resisted God's call on the grounds of some kind of imagined inadequacy. We also see this tendency in the New Testament. Jesus' response to a prospective disciple who wanted to delay answering his call so he could first attend to other business – 'No one who puts a hand to the plough and looks back is fit for the kingdom of God' (Luke 9:62) – is as unyielding as that of God's response to Jeremiah – 'Do not say, "I am only a boy"' (v. 7).

Our individual situations will be very different from that of Jeremiah, but what does remain the same is the persistence of God's call to us, whatever shape or form that call takes. But with the call comes reassurance: 'Before I formed you in the womb I knew you,' says God to Jeremiah, 'and before you were born I consecrated you' (v. 5).

How might God be calling you to follow him today?
And are you able to hear, and accept, his reassurance?

BARBARA MOSSE

Return to the Lord

A voice on the bare heights is heard, the plaintive weeping of Israel's children, because… they have forgotten the Lord their God: Return, O faithless children, I will heal your faithlessness… For thus says the Lord to the people of Judah and to the inhabitants of Jerusalem… Circumcise yourselves to the Lord, remove the foreskin of your hearts… or else my wrath will go forth like fire, and burn with no one to quench it, because of the evil of your doings.

A keen sense of sorrow and mourning pervades today's passage: the 'plaintive weeping' of the children of Israel because 'they have forgotten the Lord their God' (3:21); the pain of Jeremiah as he confronts – yet again – the stubbornness of the people; and God's pain as he reaches out in love to his beloved children. The image conjured up by the words 'return, O faithless children, I will heal your faithlessness' seems to anticipate the picture of the waiting father in Jesus' parable of the lost son (Luke 15:11–32).

But how does this picture of God as a loving father yearning for the return of his errant children fit alongside the reference to God's wrath with which our passage ends? Is God really just a stern authoritarian figure wielding a big stick? In her book *Revelations of Divine Love*, the 14th-century writer Julian of Norwich certainly didn't believe so. Her experience was that 'our Lord was never angry, nor ever shall be, for he is God… God is the goodness that cannot be angry, for he is nothing but goodness.'

Julian saw that God wasn't subject to the same vacillations of mood and temper as humans. She believed that the 'anger' we often experience, and which we attribute to God, actually lies deep within ourselves, surfacing as a natural consequence of our rebellion against the summons of divine love in our lives.

Jeremiah's message makes clear that outward religious practices need to be accompanied by an inner change of heart. In the command 'remove the foreskin of your hearts' (4:4), the Israelites are challenged to demonstrate that their commitment is, literally, more than skin-deep.

What do you think about Julian's insight, that 'God is the goodness that cannot be angry'?

BARBARA MOSSE

The ancient paths

For from the least to the greatest of them, everyone is greedy for unjust gain; and from prophet to priest, everyone deals falsely. They have treated the wound of my people carelessly, saying, 'Peace, peace', when there is no peace. They acted shamefully, they committed abomination; yet they were not ashamed, they did not know how to blush. Therefore they shall fall among those who fall; at the time that I punish them, they shall be overthrown, says the Lord. Thus says the Lord: Stand at the crossroads, and look, and ask for the ancient paths, where the good way lies; and walk in it, and find rest for your souls. But they said, 'We will not walk in it.'

When I began to think about this passage and its message to us, the contemporary sound of the sentiments expressed struck me forcibly. 'For from the least to the greatest of them, everyone is greedy for unjust gain' (v. 13) is self-evident, and screams at us from our televisions and newspapers, every day of the week. And to the church's shame, the observations the prophet makes about the religious establishment of his time also continue to have resonance: 'From prophet to priest, everyone deals falsely. They have treated the wound of my people carelessly… They committed abomination; yet they were not ashamed' (vv. 13–15).

And what is the Lord's response to all this? After the reassurance that the time will come when evil will be punished and justice will be done, the Lord's instruction may surprise us. We may be tempted to retaliate to the wrong we see around us, but God advocates a very different approach. 'Stand at the crossroads,' he says; look, and consider the different paths you could choose to follow. Take time to reflect and consider wisely. 'Ask for the ancient paths', those that have stood the test of time; and when you have found 'the good way… walk in it, and find rest for your souls' (v. 16). Calm your agitation and your outrage at the unbelievable mess we humans make of things; instead seek out the ancient ways of wisdom. These provide a safe pathway; a way of healing, refreshment and renewal.

The Israelites stubbornly chose not to follow this teaching.
What will our choice be?

BARBARA MOSSE

Let me dwell with you

The word that came to Jeremiah from the Lord: Stand in the gate of the Lord's house, and proclaim there this word, and say, Hear the word of the Lord, all you people of Judah... Thus says the Lord of hosts, the God of Israel: Amend your ways and your doings, and let me dwell with you in this place. Do not trust in these deceptive words, 'This is the temple of the Lord, the temple of the Lord, the temple of the Lord.' For... if you truly act justly one with another, if you do not oppress the alien, the orphan, and the widow, or shed innocent blood in this place, and if you do not go after other gods to your own hurt, then I will dwell with you in this place, in the land that I gave of old to your ancestors for ever and ever.

It was the American philosopher and poet Ralph Waldo Emerson (1803–82) who first coined the striking saying 'What you do speaks so loudly I can't hear what you say.' I have no memory of when I first heard this, but its power has stayed with me through the years. I was reminded of it when reading Jeremiah's prophecy from today's passage, which speaks right to the heart of the Israelites' religious practice: 'Stand in the gate of the Lord's house, and proclaim there this word' (v. 2).

The 'word' Jeremiah is being called to proclaim concerns a growing disjunction between the people's affirmation of 'the temple of the Lord' (v. 4) – repeated three times for emphasis – and the daily behaviour they routinely display, including oppression of the poor and the shedding of innocent blood. In the gospels Jesus makes a similar point when he says, 'Not everyone who says to me, "Lord, Lord", will enter the kingdom of heaven' (Matthew 7:21).

Jeremiah's reported words of the Lord come across as a plea rather than a threat: 'Amend your ways... and let me dwell with you in this place' (v. 3).

In what ways do our words in prayer and worship clash with our thoughts and actions in our everyday lives? Are we able to take the prophetic words of Jeremiah personally and accept the challenge they pose, knowing that God loves us and longs to make his home in us?

BARBARA MOSSE

They do not speak honestly

You shall say to them, Thus says the Lord: When people fall, do they not get up again? If they go astray, do they not turn back? Why then has this people turned away in perpetual backsliding? They have held fast to deceit, they have refused to return. I have given heed and listened, but they do not speak honestly; no one repents of wickedness, saying, 'What have I done!' All of them turn to their own course, like a horse plunging headlong into battle. Even the stork in the heavens knows its times; and the turtle-dove, swallow and crane observe the time of their coming; but my people do not know the ordinance of the Lord.

There is a strong strand of perversity in human nature that seems to triumph all too often, despite our best intentions and efforts. The apostle Paul was all too aware of this tendency when he lamented, 'I do not understand my own actions. For I do not do what I want, but I do the very thing I hate' (Romans 7:15). In today's passage, it seems that the spiritual state of the Israelites is even worse than Paul's description of his own situation, as it is not clear that the people even want to do the right thing. Even the birds know 'the time of their coming' (v. 7), but the people show no such discernment. And Jeremiah is given the unwelcome task of facing them with their own intransigence.

Surprisingly, perhaps, in the light of their continual disobedience, the people continue to approach God – 'I have given heed and listened' – but there is duplicity in their prayer – 'they do not speak honestly; no one repents of wickedness' (v. 6). They are approaching God with their cares and concerns, but they are doing so on their own terms, not God's. There is a presumption that the way they are choosing to behave is acceptable to, and will be endorsed by, God. They are not prepared to face up to their own disobedience, and see no need to repent.

At this point I begin to feel uncomfortable. How often do we approach God, expecting him to approve and rubber-stamp our plans? Or excuse our wrongdoing? Are we any more prepared than the Israelites were to be challenged by God?

BARBARA MOSSE

I will not listen

And the Lord said to me: Conspiracy exists among the people of Judah and the inhabitants of Jerusalem. They have turned back to the iniquities of their ancestors of old, who refused to heed my words; they have gone after other gods to serve them; the house of Israel and the house of Judah have broken the covenant that I made with their ancestors. Therefore, thus says the Lord, assuredly I am going to bring disaster upon them that they cannot escape; though they cry out to me, I will not listen to them. Then the cities of Judah and the inhabitants of Jerusalem will go and cry out to the gods to whom they make offerings, but they will never save them in the time of their trouble… As for you, do not pray for this people, or lift up a cry or prayer on their behalf, for I will not listen when they call to me in their time of trouble.

This part of Jeremiah's prophecy makes for hard, uncompromising reading. The people have violated their covenantal relationship with God time and time again, and now God's patience has finally run out. Their disobedience and faithlessness has gone too far; the Lord vows to bring disaster on them and, even more terrible, 'though they cry out to me, I will not listen to them' (v. 11). What is more, Jeremiah is forbidden to intercede on their behalf.

In the light of Jesus' later command to 'love your enemies and pray for those who persecute you' (Matthew 5:44), what are we to make of this? Perhaps the first thing to remember is that the sentiments expressed in Jeremiah's prophecy arise from within the context of a covenantal relationship between God and the Israelites. Covenants only work if both sides keep to their part of the agreement, which the Israelites have repeatedly failed to do.

The implication in this passage that there may be people or situations that we shouldn't be praying for is an uncomfortable one. Reflect today on the difficulty we have in making judgements untainted by human prejudices and preferences.

'Teach me, O Lord, the way of your statutes, and I will observe it to the end'
(Psalm 119:33).

BARBARA MOSSE

The potter and the clay

So I went down to the potter's house, and there he was working at his wheel. The vessel he was making of clay was spoiled in the potter's hand, and he reworked it into another vessel, as seemed good to him. Then the word of the Lord came to me: 'Can I not do with you, O house of Israel, just as this potter has done? says the Lord. Just like the clay in the potter's hand, so are you in my hand, O house of Israel.'

Sometimes God asks Jeremiah to 'act out' a parable in order that he may convey God's message to the people more effectively. Today's passage offers a particularly well-known example: that of the potter and the clay. The image here is used to reinforce the fact that God has sovereign power over the nation of Israel, who, despite their behaviour to the contrary, have no more autonomous power than does the clay in the hand of the potter.

What message does this passage give us if we apply its message individually? There is reassurance here, certainly. If I manage to mess up the 'clay' of my life through my sin and wrong choices, I know that God will not give up on me, but renew me, reshape me and repair the damage I have caused. But there is a warning here also, leaving no room for complacency, because the renewal and reshaping process invites my willing participation. I am not expected to be a passive observer! God's work in me asks me to listen, to cooperate with God in my daily walk with him and to allow myself to be 'worked upon' by God in the ways that he sees fit.

The key problem expressed in this prophecy of a people – or an individual – not listening to God is not new. And inevitably, we arrive at the point where the potter–clay analogy breaks down. The clay has no voice in what happens to it and cannot 'hear' the voice of its creator. But human beings have been created with hearts capable of both hearing and lovingly responding.

---

*Take a few moments today to reflect on what it feels like
to think of ourselves as clay in the hands of the potter.*

BARBARA MOSSE

Between a rock and a hard place

O Lord, you have enticed me, and I was enticed; you have overpowered me, and you have prevailed. I have become a laughing-stock all day long; everyone mocks me. For whenever I speak... I must shout 'Violence and destruction!' For the word of the Lord has become for me a reproach and derision all day long. If I say, 'I will not mention him, or speak any more in his name', then within me there is something like a burning fire shut up in my bones; I am weary with holding it in, and I cannot... Why did I come forth from the womb to see toil and sorrow, and spend my days in shame?

Jeremiah struggles continually because the message he is compelled to give is not a popular one, and it leaves him at the mercy of cruel and abusive treatment meted out by his own people (20:1–2).

We may not be called to be prophets in the same way as Jeremiah, but there is a deeper question here about the nature of our call to follow Christ, and our response to that call at different stages of our lives. Have you ever been tempted, like Jeremiah, to run away, overcome by the awesomeness of the task before you? The experience of Francis Thompson (1859–1907) in his poem 'The hound of heaven' certainly resonates with this. He describes the relentlessness of God's call in this way: 'I fled Him, down the nights and down the days... I fled Him, down the labyrinthine ways/Of my own mind; and in the midst of tears/I hid from Him.' Jeremiah may well have thought of his own experience with God in a similar way.

But at whatever age in the world's history a Christian happens to be alive on this earth, the God who loves us from all eternity is not to be avoided forever. Thompson concludes his poem with a description of God with his hand 'outstretched caressingly' saying, 'I am He Whom thou seekest!'

Jeremiah clearly feels the attraction of God's call and, at the same time, the desire to run away. In your own walk with God, do you find any points of resonance with Jeremiah's experience?

BARBARA MOSSE

Taking the long view

This is the word that came to Jeremiah from the Lord, when King Zedekiah sent to him Pashhur son of Malchiah… saying, 'Please inquire of the Lord on our behalf, for King Nebuchadnezzar of Babylon is making war against us…' Thus says the Lord: See, I am setting before you the way of life and the way of death. Those who stay in this city shall die by the sword, by famine, and by pestilence; but those who go out and surrender to the Chaldeans who are besieging you shall live and shall have their lives as a prize of war. For I have set my face against this city for evil and not for good… It shall be given into the hands of the king of Babylon, and he shall burn it with fire.

Pashhur has already been warned that Judah will be taken captive into Babylon (20:4); this was not the answer he wanted, so he asks again, obviously hoping for a more favourable response. There is no change, however. Rather the stern judgement of God is repeated with further emphasis, with the warning that 'I myself will fight against you with outstretched hand and mighty arm' (21:5).

The clear-cut choice between life and death is a familiar one in the Old Testament, particularly in the Psalms. The problem here in Jeremiah is that the way the people were being asked to choose – yes to exile, no to staying and fighting – must have seemed the very opposite of what they felt they should do. Surely the land God had given them and the holy city of Jerusalem should be defended at all costs?

Looking back over many centuries of hindsight, we know that the experience of exile was vital for the nation, and that through it the people's relationship with God deepened and matured. But it can't have seemed like that at the time. How do we respond when things happen that appear – to us – to be the very opposite of what we imagine God's will to be?

Do you have any experience of situations when the direction God seems to be pointing appears to go against everything you would expect? How were you able to use the gift of discernment in such situations?

BARBARA MOSSE

Baskets of figs

The Lord showed me two baskets of figs… And the Lord said to me, 'What do you see, Jeremiah?' I said, 'Figs, the good figs very good, and the bad figs… so bad that they cannot be eaten.'… Thus says the Lord… Like these good figs, so I will regard as good the exiles from Judah, whom I have sent away from this place to the land of the Chaldeans… I will bring them back to this land… for they shall return to me with their whole heart. But thus says the Lord: Like the bad figs that are so bad they cannot be eaten, so will I treat King Zedekiah of Judah, his officials, the remnant of Jerusalem who remain in this land… I will make them a horror, an evil thing, to all the kingdoms of the earth.

The message of this prophecy, using another of Jeremiah's visual parables, reinforces the message of yesterday's text. The instruction about God's will concerning the conflict between Judah and the Babylonians is so counter-intuitive it is reinforced by a strong image. Things could not be made any clearer: the basket of good figs refers to those who allow themselves to be vanquished and taken into captivity; and the bad – 'so bad that they could not be eaten' (v. 2) – to those who resist the Babylonian enemy and stay behind in Jerusalem.

The people were not able to see that the traumatic experience of exile was to be a vital stage of growth in their relationship with God. Only Jeremiah had the clarity of vision and the closeness to God to discern accurately the path ahead. He knew that the medicine would taste bitter, but the nation needed to swallow it in order to be restored to full health and a right relationship to God.

Part of Jeremiah's prophetic role was to listen to God on behalf of the nation, to discern the will of God and to communicate that will in a way that the people could understand.

As our own Christian journey continues to unfold, are we prepared to take time to listen deeply to God and to take on our part in the process of discernment?

BARBARA MOSSE

Accepting exile

These are the words of the letter that the prophet Jeremiah sent from Jerusalem to the remaining elders among the exiles... Thus says the Lord of hosts, the God of Israel, to all the exiles whom I have sent into exile from Jerusalem to Babylon: Build houses and live in them; plant gardens and eat what they produce. Take wives and have sons and daughters; take wives for your sons, and give your daughters in marriage... But seek the welfare of the city where I have sent you into exile, and pray to the Lord on its behalf, for in its welfare you will find your welfare.

The worst has happened, and Jeremiah's prophetic warnings of catastrophe have been fulfilled. The message in today's text is for 'the remaining elders among the exiles' (v. 1), to be communicated to the people in general. It is not difficult to imagine the state of mind among the exiles: traumatised, bereaved, fearful, hearts aching for home.

There is a marked change from the tone of the earlier prophecies. Gone is the sense of urgency and the dire warnings of death and destruction. Instead there is a sense of calm, quiet and reassurance. Settle down, says God, and stop fretting about your lost homeland; you are in this for the long haul. Build houses, plant gardens, marry and, a generation down the line, arrange marriages for your children. Most significantly, and in anticipation of Jesus' later instruction to 'love your enemies and pray for those who persecute you' (Matthew 5:44), the people are urged to pray for Babylon and its welfare, because their own health and happiness is inextricably connected with that of the Babylonians.

There is a clear message here about the need to live in the present moment. How much of our time do we spend dreaming of a future that we think will somehow be better than the reality of our present circumstances? It is here, in the mess or sheer ordinariness of our daily lives, that God is to be encountered, rather than in some idealised future.

Spend some time today reflecting on these words of Jesus:
'So do not worry about tomorrow, for tomorrow will bring worries of its own. Today's trouble is enough for today' (Matthew 6:34).

BARBARA MOSSE

The promise of restoration

The word of the Lord came to Jeremiah a second time, while he was still confined in the court of the guard... Call to me and I will answer you, and will tell you great and hidden things that you have not known... I am going to bring [this city] recovery and healing; I will heal them and reveal to them abundance of prosperity and security. I will restore the fortunes of Judah and the fortunes of Israel, and rebuild them as they were at first. I will cleanse them from all the guilt of their sin against me, and I will forgive all the guilt of their sin and rebellion against me.

Jeremiah's prophecies have revealed an unfolding pattern. Through them, the people have been rebuked for their faithless behaviour, warned of the consequences, encouraged to accept exile, and urged to put down roots and live with the present moment and all it has to offer. It seems that, beyond the indignity of exile, life for the people in Babylon is actually quite good; they have freedom of movement and are able to live their lives without undue constraint.

Jeremiah, however, has no such freedom, as he has been left behind in Jerusalem and confined in the court of the guard. It may seem surprising, then, that this prophecy, given in such grim circumstances, carries such a wholehearted message of promise. And we at last begin to see more clearly the end that God has always had in view: the complete recovery and healing of the dispersed houses of Judah and Israel, with cleansing and forgiveness for all their sin.

This encouragement to seek – and trust that we will find – the light in the darkest of situations that we may encounter is a thread that runs throughout scripture, from the earliest disaster in the garden of Eden to the final consummation of all things at the end of time.

So often, 'we see through a glass, darkly' (1 Corinthians 13:12, KJV) and struggle to trust that there is anything beyond the current difficulty. Reflect for a few moments on your own experience in such situations, and on the promise that scripture offers us of 'the assurance of things hoped for, the conviction of things not seen' (Hebrews 11:1).

BARBARA MOSSE

They did not listen

The word that came to Jeremiah for all the Judeans living in the land of Egypt, at Migdol, at Tahpanhes, at Memphis, and in the land of Pathros, Thus says the Lord of hosts, the God of Israel: You yourselves have seen all the disaster that I have brought on Jerusalem and on all the towns of Judah. Look at them; today they are a desolation, without an inhabitant in them, because of the wickedness they committed, provoking me to anger, in that they went to make offerings and serve other gods that they had not known, neither they, nor you, nor your ancestors. Yet I persistently sent to you all my servants the prophets, saying, 'I beg you not to do this abominable thing that I hate!' But they did not listen or incline their ear, to turn away from their wickedness and make no offerings to other gods.

As we come to today's reading, we may feel some sense of disorientation. It is clear that a considerable length of time has passed, because those Judeans who remained behind in Jerusalem with Jeremiah have now scattered and are to be found in four cities in Egypt (Migdol, Tahpanhes, Memphis and Pathros). But despite the changes of location, it seems that not much has changed in terms of the people's relationship to God. Idolatry and continued disobedience still feature prominently in the divine complaint. Jeremiah's prophetic messages of warning also continue – the disaster visited on Jerusalem because of the nation's persistent idolatry is held up as an object lesson, a natural consequence of the people's persistent refusal to listen to God.

These long-ago events are very distant from our own experience. But let us examine for a moment the recurring complaint in these prophecies: 'they did not listen or incline their ear' (v. 5). In our churches and fellowships we hear a great deal about the depths of God's love; not so much, perhaps, about the reality of sin and God's judgement. It's a delicate balance, but both elements have their place. Related to both is the injunction to listen to God – as a nation, as churches and as individuals.

Reflect for a few moments today on the ways your church enables –
or fails to enable – people to listen to God.

BARBARA MOSSE

Divine wisdom

Thus says the Lord: I am going to stir up a destructive wind against Babylon… It is [the Lord] who made the earth by his power, who established the world by his wisdom, and by his understanding stretched out the heavens… He makes lightnings for the rain, and he brings out the wind from his storehouses. Everyone is stupid and without knowledge; goldsmiths are all put to shame by their idols; for their images are false, and there is no breath in them. They are worthless, a work of delusion; at the time of their punishment they shall perish. Not like these is the Lord, the portion of Jacob, for he is the one who formed all things, and Israel is the tribe of his inheritance; the Lord of hosts is his name.

The final chapter of the book of Jeremiah consists of an intense diatribe against Babylon. It's payback time with a vengeance, as the Lord promises to punish Babylon for its treatment of Judah and its people. The cumulative effect of the developing prophetic argument leaves us with an overwhelming impression of the sheer power and majesty of God, whose ways and thoughts are so very different from our own (Isaiah 55:8).

We have journeyed some considerable distance with Jeremiah over the past few days. We have accompanied him from his reluctant response to God's call, through the pain he experienced on account of the message he had to deliver and the people's hostility to him when he delivered that message. We stayed with him when he was imprisoned in Jerusalem, still sending his prophetic messages to the exiles in Babylon.

As we conclude our journey, we may still find we are left with questions about the mysterious workings of God, and how God relates to those who seek to follow him. But above and beyond all our questioning, we are invited to trust that God indeed 'established the world by his wisdom' (v. 15), and that, with Israel, we are 'the tribe of his inheritance' (v. 19).

The second verse of the hymn 'Alleluia, Sing to Jesus' contains the line, 'Faith believes, nor questions how'. What place do you think our questions have in the development of a mature faith?

BARBARA MOSSE

My favourite prayers

If you are anything like me, you pray using words in a variety of ways. Sometimes I chat to God informally, as I might with people at work or while pottering at home. On other occasions I petition God with prayers of intercession for personal or wider needs. This is the case on hearing the news or when thinking about particular people or circumstances. Throughout the day there are prayers of thanksgiving and repentance. As well as saying prayers before meals, I have a tradition of offering thank you, please and sorry prayers at the end of each day: that is, I thank God for at least five things, make two or three requests, either for myself or for others, and then say one prayer of confession. Such prayers are of the moment and are not recorded in any form.

I also enjoy praying prayers written by other people. My favourite ones are seasonal, not in terms of spring or summer but of the seasons of life. I have found that certain prayers 'seek me out' – they appear frequently over a period of days or weeks in something I am reading or listening to, or a friend happens to mention the prayer at that time. It can feel as if God is inviting me to address a specific theme in life. (For example, my awareness of older people grew when I discovered the prayer I have chosen for Tuesday is the favourite of each member of a group comprising individuals aged 90 and above.) Hence the prayers I have chosen for the next seven days are not necessarily those I might have picked some months ago, nor will they be the same in a year or so.

The selection includes liturgical prayers, some of which have been used for centuries in one form or another. It can be a huge relief to use words honed by sages, to express what I think and feel, whether or not I am alongside others as I do so. In response, my own thoughts, words and actions will follow. May it be so as you speak to and listen to God.

LAKSHMI JEFFREYS

God knows

O Lord, you have searched me and known me. You know when I sit down and when I rise up; you discern my thoughts from far away. You search out my path and my lying down, and are acquainted with all my ways. Even before a word is on my tongue, O Lord, you know it completely.

'I prayed, but it didn't work.' People cry out, at times in hope and on other occasions in despair, but it seems what they want does not come about. Perhaps the problem is not the prayers themselves. Sometimes the person praying has lost sight of, or maybe has yet to encounter, the God to whom the prayers are addressed. God can become a parental figure who wants the best for us but does not give anything. On the other hand, there are people aware of God's omnipotence who cannot believe this God is interested in their own daily existence. In either case, prayer can feel like putting a request in a slot machine that does not deliver.

Assuming David wrote this psalm, here was a man well aware of the God addressed in prayer. Yet even David is overwhelmed by God's intimate knowledge of him. The God who has on countless occasions rescued his people from their enemies; the God whose name is so special it cannot be spoken: this God knows every action, thought, hope and word of David – or of you or me.

Holding the tension between God's enormity and intimacy is a challenge. St Augustine manages it beautifully in what has become the collect (prayer to draw together the silent prayers of a congregation) for Trinity 17.

Change 'our' to 'my', 'us' to 'me' and so on in the prayer below:
*   'Almighty God,*
*   you have made us for yourself,*
*   and our hearts are restless*
*   till they find their rest in you:*
*   pour your love into our hearts*
*   and draw us to yourself,*
*   and so bring us at last to your heavenly city*
*   where we shall see you face-to-face;*
*   through Jesus Christ, your Son, our Lord' (Collect for Trinity 17).*

LAKSHMI JEFFREYS

Agent and endpoint

He is the image of the invisible God, the firstborn of all creation; for in him all things in heaven and on earth were created, things visible and invisible... All things have been created through him and for him. He himself is before all things, and in him all things hold together. He is the head of the body, the church; he is the beginning, the firstborn from the dead, so that he might come to have first place in everything. For in him all the fullness of God was pleased to dwell, and through him God was pleased to reconcile to himself all things, whether on earth or in heaven, by making peace through the blood of his cross.

Having been reminded yesterday of the intimacy of the creator God, the focus today is on Jesus. The passage expresses how Jesus shows us what God is like, fully representing God. He is both an agent of creation and its endpoint, holding the whole of creation together. At the same time Jesus is the origin and principal of the church, as well as the living Lord who has overcome death. As a result of Jesus' death and resurrection, God has made peace with creation, including all people. Hence Jesus will present us before God, holy and blameless. In Hebrews, we are told that Jesus intercedes for us at God's right hand.

Because of who Jesus is and what Jesus has done and is doing, we can respond in words and actions. Jesus is on our side, meaning we can come before him exactly as we are, to be healed and inspired to love.

Love for God is always expressed in love for neighbour.
How might this look for you today?

'Almighty God,
to whom all hearts are open,
all desires known,
and from whom no secrets are hidden:
cleanse the thoughts of our hearts
by the inspiration of your Holy Spirit,
that we may perfectly love you,
and worthily magnify your holy name;
through Christ our Lord' (Collect for Purity).

LAKSHMI JEFFREYS

True sight

As [Jesus] walked along, he saw a man blind from birth. His disciples asked him, 'Rabbi, who sinned, this man or his parents, that he was born blind?' Jesus answered, 'Neither this man nor his parents sinned; he was born blind so that God's works might be revealed in him... As long as I am in the world, I am the light of the world.' When he had said this, he spat on the ground and made mud with the saliva and spread the mud on the man's eyes, saying to him, 'Go, wash in the pool of Siloam' (which means Sent). Then he went and washed and came back able to see.

Since I wear contact lenses, most people have little idea of how poor my eyesight is. At the same time, when wearing lenses I need glasses for any close work. Good light, however, makes a significant difference, so that I can sometimes read or sew without having to hunt for and then wear my glasses. I am still surprised at how anxious I feel when I cannot see clearly and at the extraordinary relief that comes when I am in better light.

John's gospel is full of imagery, including sight and blindness, light and dark. The man, born blind, is able to see when he obeys Jesus, the light of the world. In the story following today's passage, the religious leaders, although physically able to see, are blind to the things of God, unable to accept Jesus. There is a blindness of will that Jesus' light will penetrate when we are able to submit to his authority and trust him. Sadly, if we fear being open to Jesus, we remain blind to the things of God.

Most people experience physical fear, but also less tangible anxiety. Jesus is able to shed light to show us how things really are, if we are willing to ask him.

Where are the dark areas in your life requiring Jesus' light?
'Lighten our darkness, we beseech thee, O Lord; and by thy great mercy defend us from all perils and dangers of this night; for the love of thy only Son, our Saviour, Jesus Christ' (Book of Common Prayer, 1928).

LAKSHMI JEFFREYS

Responding to God

The angel Gabriel was sent by God… And he came to her and said, 'Greetings, favoured one! The Lord is with you… Do not be afraid, Mary, for you have found favour with God. And now, you will conceive in your womb and bear a son, and you will name him Jesus. He will be great, and will be called the Son of the Most High… and of his kingdom there will be no end.' Mary said to the angel, 'How can this be, since I am a virgin?' The angel said to her, 'The Holy Spirit will come upon you, and the power of the Most High will overshadow you; therefore the child to be born will be holy; he will be called Son of God…' Then Mary said, 'Here am I, the servant of the Lord; let it be with me according to your word.'

I have a friend whose catchphrase is, 'You have a choice.' A superficial reading of the annunciation might cause us to wonder if Mary could really have said, 'No, thank you.' If so, she would not have been the first: Moses, Gideon, Isaiah and countless others doubted their ability to undertake the task for which God called them. Even Mary questioned the likelihood of a virgin having a baby before she graciously accepted her place in God's plan.

It takes courage to be open to God's invitation, and it is important to remember that, however we feel about ourselves, God does not make mistakes. Choosing to say yes to God will bring Jesus' promise of life in all its fullness (John 10:10).

'Father, I abandon myself into your hands; do with me what you will. Whatever you may do, I thank you: I am ready for all, I accept all. Let only your will be done in me, and in all your creatures – I wish no more than this, O Lord. Into your hands I commend my soul: I offer it to you with all the love of my heart, for I love you, Lord, and so need to give myself, to surrender myself into your hands without reserve, and with boundless confidence, for you are my Father' (Charles de Foucauld).

LAKSHMI JEFFREYS

Honest faith

And they brought the boy to [Jesus]. When the spirit saw him, immediately it threw the boy into convulsions, and he fell on the ground and rolled about, foaming at the mouth. Jesus asked the father, 'How long has this been happening to him?' And he said, 'From childhood. It has often cast him into the fire and into the water, to destroy him; but if you are able to do anything, have pity on us and help us.' Jesus said to him, 'If you are able! – All things can be done for the one who believes.' Immediately the father of the child cried out, 'I believe; help my unbelief!'

The father of the boy brought to Jesus could do nothing to help his son. The child had been afflicted all his life. 'If you are able to do anything, have pity on us and help us,' his father says (v. 22). He wants Jesus to do something, yet he is not sure. He longs to trust Jesus but has responsibility for his child. There is tension between the father's desire to make his son better and his faith in Jesus.

Janice usually prayed faithfully for herself and others. When her mother was dying, at one level Janice knew that Jesus would bring healing, peace and the ability to cope, but she struggled to find ten minutes to spend with him.

Dan hated his job, but redundancy would mean a change of lifestyle. Yet on the leadership team at his church, Dan had been instrumental in praying for and highlighting God's provision.

Sam and Jo knew God loved their daughter even more than they did, but it was so difficult to trust God with the young woman during the latest crisis.

I wonder if faith is like a muscle that needs to be exercised to grow stronger? Many of us want to trust God but cannot let go of our need to manage our way – even if we really have no control. Faith involves trusting God with what we want to control and then acting as if God loves and wants the best for us – however tentative our belief. Jesus answered the father's desperate prayer – and he will answer yours and mine.

'I believe; help my unbelief!' (v. 24).

LAKSHMI JEFFREYS

Living well

'Where then does wisdom come from? And where is the place of under-standing? It is hidden from the eyes of all living, and concealed from the birds of the air. Abaddon and Death say, "We have heard a rumour of it with our ears." God understands the way to it, and he knows its place. For he looks to the ends of the earth, and sees everything under the heavens… And he said to humankind, "Truly, the fear of the Lord, that is wisdom; and to depart from evil is understanding."'

The best leaders hold a vision for the organisation they lead and are able to stay calm, remaining true to themselves in the presence of conflict and sabotage. They are so clear on who they are that they have nothing to prove to anyone. That sense of clarity is most apparent in individuals who know they are loved and accepted as they are. Perhaps that is why 'the fear of the Lord is the beginning of wisdom' (Proverbs 9:10). If we are aware that God loves us because of who he has created us to be and that God wants the best for us, we have no need to justify ourselves to anyone; even death will hold no fear for us.

Knowing that it is God who gives and takes away life, Job discovers that the source of wisdom is not a philosophical idea but a relationship with this God. Wisdom, the fear of the Lord, is to be in awe of who God is. Understanding is perhaps wisdom in action, to do what God says and depart from evil. Jesus said that whoever loved him would do what he said.

When we truly listen to God, we sometimes discover we are the answer to our own prayers. When asked why God didn't do anything to stop war, evil, famine and homelessness, the wise minister answered, 'God did something: he created you and me.'

'Teach us, dear Lord, to number our days;
that we may apply our hearts unto wisdom.
Oh, satisfy us early with Thy mercy,
that we may rejoice and be glad all of our days.
And let the beauty of the Lord our God be upon us;
and establish Thou the work of our hands, dear Lord'
(Canticle from Northumbria Community's Midday Prayer).

LAKSHMI JEFFREYS

All shall be well

'See, the home of God is among mortals. He will dwell with them; they will be his peoples, and God himself will be with them; he will wipe every tear from their eyes. Death will be no more; mourning and crying and pain will be no more, for the first things have passed away.' And the one who was seated on the throne said, 'See, I am making all things new.'

'All shall be well and all shall be well and all manner of things shall be well': so said Julian of Norwich. Having come close to death, Julian had nothing to fear (see yesterday's note), and whatever happened she had no doubt that God remained the God of love, with all that followed.

While these words from Revelation will be fully realised in heaven, the kingdom of God – the rule of God over all things – has already begun. Through the Holy Spirit, God dwells with his people. Christians are never called to live in isolation and, as we trust God with ourselves, so we can experience comfort and transformation. While death, mourning, crying and pain are still around, they are not the end; there is hope.

At the time of writing, it is the anniversary of my father's death and my mother is receiving end-of-life care. The reality of the words of Julian, as well as those of St Teresa, below, is powerful because the one in heaven is making all things new. He is the one who hears and responds to our prayers; who loves us to death – and beyond; who remains with us by the Holy Spirit; who will show us how to be the answer to many of our own prayers; and who will grow in us patience to wait for his full response.

As you read the last of my (current) favourite prayers, I invite you to sit with each line before the living God in heaven, aware that he is the beginning and the end and, whatever you face, with him all shall be well.

'Let nothing disturb you,
let nothing frighten you,
all things will pass away.
God never changes;
patience obtains all things,
whoever has God lacks nothing.
God alone suffices' (Teresa of Avila).

LAKSHMI JEFFREYS

Women in the New Testament

Missionaries have a saying: 'There is no gospel before culture.' By this they mean that the gospel is not preached into a cultural vacuum, and the preacher is not uninfluenced by their home culture. Wherever the gospel is preached, it arrives from the evangelists' culture to be received into the hearers' different culture. It is thus important to bear in mind, as we come to the scriptures, that the gospel, originally Jewish in culture, was preached in the context of, and to some extent was influenced by, the other cultures that were significant in first-century Palestine.

Our scriptures open with two creation stories. The first describes the creation of humanity in God's image as male and female – suggesting equality and a basis for accepting nature's gender variations. The second has woman created from man's rib as 'an help meet' (Genesis 2:18, KJV) – an equal partner of identical substance, close to his heart.

Then comes the fall, with its loss of harmony and innocence, the beginning of struggle and sorrow. God curses humanity, saying to Eve that she will bring forth children in pain, desiring her husband yet ruled over by him. Adam's sin is identified as listening to the voice of his wife. The relationship shifts towards dominance and subjugation. Tragically, we have seen many instances over the centuries of people using this episode as a justification for the silencing of, and domination over, women by men.

Observing the attitudes and responses of Jesus and then of Paul, we realise that part of our salvation is the restoration of equality: 'There is no longer Jew or Greek, there is no longer slave or free, there is no longer male and female; for all of you are one in Christ Jesus' (Galatians 3:28, NRSV). The vision is restored of a God of love containing and originating the beauty and variety of both male and female, with a corresponding imperative to honour and respect all humanity. Yet the challenge this presents to societal norms is to be undertaken quietly, gently, gracefully and with propriety, as befits the Christian way. In these studies of women in the New Testament, we see something of that in action.

PENELOPE WILCOCK

Lydia of Thyatira

A certain woman named Lydia, a worshipper of God, was listening to us; she was from the city of Thyatira and a dealer in purple cloth. The Lord opened her heart to listen eagerly to what was said by Paul. When she and her household were baptized, she urged us, saying, 'If you have judged me to be faithful to the Lord, come and stay at my home.' And she prevailed upon us.

Lydia came from a Greek city in what is now western Turkey, so her background is Gentile. She must have been a convert to Judaism, because Paul found her with other women assembled at a riverside *proseuchē* (translated as 'place of prayer', the word typically used for a synagogue) just outside Philippi's city gates. It was usual for Paul to begin missionary work in a new place at the local synagogue, so we can assume that to be the case here.

Paul did not wait or look for male devotees, but was happy to begin sharing the gospel with this group of women. Lydia seems to have a leading role, perhaps because her business dealing in expensive cloth gave her high social status.

She also commands her household; there is no mention of her deferring to a husband. When she enthusiastically and happily receives the word of the gospel, she has the power to offer hospitality to the missionaries and introduce the good news about Jesus to all those under her roof.

From the story of Lydia, we know that women held independent positions of leadership respected by the apostles. She also models for us an attitude of freedom and confidence in her eagerness for spiritual wisdom, her glad recognition of the truth of Paul's message and her open, welcoming hospitality.

Am I eager for spiritual truth? How can I make my heart, my home and my life more open to the power of the gospel?

Open my heart, living God, to the inspiration of the Holy Spirit. May the doors of my home stand open to those who bring your gospel. May I and my household ever serve the truth and love of Jesus. Amen

PENELOPE WILCOCK

Dorcas of Joppa

All the widows stood beside him, weeping and showing tunics and other clothing that Dorcas had made while she was with them. Peter put all of them outside, and then he knelt down and prayed. He turned to the body and said, 'Tabitha, get up.' Then she opened her eyes, and seeing Peter, she sat up. He gave her his hand and helped her up. Then calling the saints and widows, he showed her to be alive.

Dorcas (also known as Tabitha), a seamstress and a disciple in the new Christian Way, was known for doing good and helping the poor. When she died after a short illness, it was not children or a husband who mourned her loss, but the widows in her home town of Joppa. Dorcas herself may also have been a widow, or she may have never married.

The story brings out some social realities. The widows of Joppa are likely to have been among those in poverty who depended on Dorcas' help and kindness, yet she herself was evidently not poor or in need. In those days (and still today) women were among society's more vulnerable members, their home and income often dependent on male relatives, their lives plunged into destitution on a husband's death. But a wealthy single woman, whose finances had no family obligations, could lift out of poverty the other women whose situation she well understood.

Peter was called upon not for his male privilege in society, but because of his spiritual power that came from walking close with Jesus. Through him, God gave them back what they needed – another woman like themselves, a sister who understood.

Among those in need, with whom do I especially connect? Who among God's poor quickens my sense of fellow-feeling? Where can I make a difference, and be a true friend to someone on the margins?

Jesus, carpenter of Nazareth, friend of the poor, give me humility to work with my hands and compassion to use my resources for good. May my life bless those who struggle, extending the reach of your kingdom. Amen

PENELOPE WILCOCK

Priscilla of Corinth

Apollos… was an eloquent man, well-versed in the scriptures. He had been instructed in the Way of the Lord; and he spoke with burning enthusiasm and taught accurately the things concerning Jesus, though he knew only the baptism of John. He began to speak boldly in the synagogue; but when Priscilla and Aquila heard him, they took him aside and explained the Way of God to him more accurately.

The apostle Paul first met Priscilla and Aquila at Corinth, on his second missionary journey. They had just moved there from Italy. He lived and worked with them for 18 months, after which they travelled with him to Ephesus, where this incident with Apollos happened.

Priscilla and Aquila are mentioned six times in the New Testament, always together; on four occasions, unconventionally, Priscilla's name comes before Aquila's. This may suggest that her ministry was of particular significance. We know that they risked their lives for Paul, and that the local church met in their home (see Romans 16:3–5).

We see in their interaction with Apollos that their ministry is held jointly and their leadership shared. Priscilla is not 'the vicar's wife' but a co-worker with Aquila in establishing and building up the church. She has a teaching role on a basis equal to her husband's, with the authority to correct and instruct men.

In this passage, where we see the two of them at work, what stands out is their kindness and discretion. They don't argue with Apollos or show him up in front of those gathered at the synagogue. They take him aside quietly to explain the aspects of discipleship where he still has something to learn. This tiny vignette of church leadership speaks volumes about how to connect effectively, how to nurture discipleship and how to correct others without humiliating them or dampening their enthusiasm.

With whom am I most comfortable working together in ministry? Where do the relationships in my life especially require tact and kindness?

Jesus, you were always kind, though you taught with authority.
Give me confidence to speak out your truth, but give me restraint as well.
May I, like you, be gentle. Amen

PENELOPE WILCOCK

Sapphira of Jerusalem

A man named Ananias, with the consent of his wife Sapphira, sold a piece of property; with his wife's knowledge, he kept back some of the proceeds, and brought only a part and laid it at the apostles' feet. 'Ananias,' Peter asked, 'why has Satan filled your heart to lie to the Holy Spirit and to keep back part of the proceeds of the land?'… When Ananias heard these words, he… died.

Our passage is an extract from the story of Ananias and Sapphira. You might like to read the whole account (Acts 5:1–11) to understand that Peter's indignation is not due to the couple's withholding money but because they pretended to have donated the whole amount when really they kept back part of the proceeds. After Ananias falls dead, Sapphira arrives at the meeting and independently maintains the lie. She, like her husband, is struck dead. Unsurprisingly, this makes a big impression on the assembled church!

It's a depressingly sordid little tale of the human desire to look good and our willingness to connive at suppressing truth – but what can we learn from it? I suggest two main things.

First, that honesty and transparency are foundational to the health of the church. The dismal tales of covert child abuse in modern times are instances of how corruption and focusing on preserving appearances rot the faith community from within and sever the arteries of its spiritual power. Unless we live the truth we proclaim, who will believe us?

Second, we see that Peter holds Sapphira separately and equally accountable for the couple's decision-making. She is a responsible adult in her own right. As the church developed, teaching about male headship and female submission resulted in the faith community losing hold of the free and responsible spirituality of women. In its sombre lesson, the story of Sapphira reminds us that God sees women as accountable equals to men.

God of truth, sift my heart. Set me free from prevarication and pretence. May I be a trustworthy disciple, an honest Christian with no part in guile or deceit. May others always be able to rely upon my word. Amen

PENELOPE WILCOCK

Junia of Rome

Greet Prisca and Aquila, who work with me in Christ Jesus, and who risked their necks for my life, to whom not only I give thanks, but also all the churches of the Gentiles. Greet also the church in their house… Greet Mary, who has worked very hard among you. Greet Andronicus and Junia, my relatives who were in prison with me; they are prominent among the apostles, and they were in Christ before I was.

Our fleeting glimpse of Junia in the letter to the Romans has given rise to a surprising level of controversy. Why? Because she was a woman. Some scholars have proposed that a woman could not have been a prominent apostle, so the name must really have been Junias (male, but problematically unknown in the ancient Greek world). The tweak lingers wistfully in footnotes. Others say that since Junia was clearly a woman, 'apostle' here cannot mean what it usually does, but instead merely denotes a messenger. The scholars opting for the masculine form of the name are content with the description of a prominent apostle.

The argument becomes less important once we acknowledge (as did fourth-century John Chrysostom) that Junia was an apostle both prominent (or outstanding) and female. Though it is puzzling to balance this with some of Paul's teaching on limiting female authority, it is important we recognise that nowhere does the New Testament teach that women cannot be church leaders, apostles or missionaries; rather, it makes apparent that they were.

What can we learn from this? We can acquire the habit of questioning and probing cultural assumptions that have become entrenched in church life as though they were tenets of the gospel. The steady progression of emancipation and enlightenment is often fictional. The Church Fathers accepted Junia's prominence as an apostle without question; only in subsequent years did commentators try to discredit her. The challenge for us is to look at the contemporary world through the biblical lens, not to try to impose the viewpoint of modern society on to the Bible.

God of truth, give me grace to look and wisdom to see.
Make me, in reality and fullness, a Bible Christian. Amen

PENELOPE WILCOCK

Phoebe of Cenchreae

I commend to you our sister Phoebe, a deacon of the church at Cenchreae, so that you may welcome her in the Lord as is fitting for the saints, and help her in whatever she may require from you, for she has been a benefactor of many and of myself as well... Greet Philologus, Julia, Nereus and his sister, and Olympas, and all the saints who are with them.

This mention of Phoebe as a church deacon is important in challenging suppositions that church leadership must be male. Where they planted churches, the apostles would appoint elders and a deacon from the first (so most seasoned) converts. Deacons ranked below apostles and elders but held a leadership role, implying authority as well as pastoral care.

In the apostle Paul's instructions about deacons in 1 Timothy 3:8–13 (interestingly, also the letter in which Paul forbids women to have authority over men) they are assumed to be male; yet here Paul commends Phoebe's ministry. This leadership role would have been a permanent position in church governance, to ensure stability and to guard against the incursion of heresy. The person in post would, therefore, have had a good grasp of theology and a steady, trustworthy character. Our passage suggests Phoebe added to this the characteristics of generosity and encouragement – 'she has been a benefactor of many' (v. 2).

Our passage also mentions Julia, included not as a wife or sister but in her own right. Evidently respect for the ministry of women was alive and well in Paul's mind.

The lesson for us, perhaps, is to be willing to live with unresolved issues, to keep an open mind. Why does Paul commend Phoebe's ministry to the Romans but tell Timothy he does not permit women to exercise authority over men? Did his understanding change as it developed? Were his permissions relative to cultural norms in each church's context? Living at peace with unanswered questions is part of the art of discipleship.

Be our teacher, our shepherd, our guide, loving God; and as we journey with you, keep our minds open to new perspectives. May we be steadfast, but not rigid, in our faith. Amen

PENELOPE WILCOCK

Euodia and Syntyche

Therefore, my brothers and sisters, whom I love and long for, my joy and crown, stand firm in the Lord… I urge Euodia and I urge Syntyche to be of the same mind in the Lord. Yes, and I ask you also, my loyal companion, help these women, for they have struggled beside me in the work of the gospel, together with Clement and the rest of my co-workers, whose names are in the book of life.

Euodia and Syntyche were considerable individuals. Paul describes them as struggling alongside him; they have worked vigorously and faithfully to extend the reach of the gospel. We don't know the specifics of the struggle, but the fact that some translations use the word 'contended' instead of 'struggled' suggests it involved missionary activity and apologetics. Paul includes these women with his co-workers – like Timothy and Epaphroditus – together with Clement here.

Why does Paul urge them to be of the same mind? Does he mean that they should be in agreement with what he's been saying, or does he mean that they should be reconciled with each other? Where strong personalities work together in leadership, there is often a clash. If that's so here, one might wonder if Euodia and Syntyche, reading the letter, were tempted to respond, 'Ha! Sort out your own arguments, mate!' Paul certainly had some serious disagreements himself. Did these two women lock horns in their exercise of church leadership?

What can we learn from these two women in the church at Philippi? How comfortably do I fit into my own church community? How do I respond to conflict? Do I withdraw, become antagonistic or try to talk things through? Do I seek the company of others who see life as I do, or get along happily with people of differing points of view? In what ways do I struggle for the work of the gospel? How do I help and encourage my own church leaders?

You see all my ways, wise and loving God. Encourage me where I am timid, restrain me where I am overbearing, calm me where I am touchy. By your grace may my name be written with Euodia's and Syntyche's in the book of life. Amen

PENELOPE WILCOCK

Chloe of Corinth

Now I appeal to you, brothers and sisters, by the name of our Lord Jesus Christ, that all of you should be in agreement and that there should be no divisions among you, but that you should be united in the same mind and the same purpose. For it has been reported to me by Chloe's people that there are quarrels among you, my brothers and sisters.

Who was Chloe? We know so little about her. Yet 'Chloe's people' (v. 11) implies it was she who had the personal connection with Paul, rather than the people who visited him, or he would have mentioned by name those who spoke to him. The phrase also suggests they were her subordinates. It seems likely she was leader of one of the churches that met in the homes of influential Christians; house churches were the New Testament norm, and women led and hosted some of these. Perhaps those reporting to Paul were sent as a delegation by Chloe. That they alerted Paul to the divisions suggests they themselves felt dismayed by the development and did not represent one of the factions. We are told so little about Chloe, yet can conjecture a certain amount even from one tiny phrase.

What can we learn from this? It speaks of the priority of church unity for the early church leaders. Jesus' intercessory prayer in John 17 pleads and advocates for unity, and the book of Acts records the often painful process of finding ways to hold the church together as Gentile converts flood in to join the new movement, developing it beyond its Jewish roots. Wherever there is more than one person in a room, sooner or later there will be differences of opinion. The cross, the self-sacrifice required of us in following Jesus, has to do with embracing one another in love even as we speak up in honesty for what we believe in our hearts to be true. Division is the blight of Christian witness.

God of love and unity, three in one, you call us to walk in reconciliation and peace. Give us, we pray, both the skills and the resolve we shall need for this even to be possible; for Jesus' sake. Amen

PENELOPE WILCOCK

Apphia of Colossae

Paul, a prisoner of Christ Jesus, and Timothy our brother, To Philemon our dear friend and co-worker, to Apphia our sister, to Archippus our fellow-soldier, and to the church in your house: Grace to you and peace from God our Father and the Lord Jesus Christ. When I remember you in my prayers, I always thank my God because I hear of your love for all the saints and your faith towards the Lord Jesus.

Paul's letter to Philemon is a masterpiece of diplomacy. Paul writes to say that he is sending back to Philemon his escaped slave Onesimus, who has now become a Christian, and to plead for mercy for the runaway.

Though personal in tone, the letter is not just private correspondence between Paul and Philemon, as we see when we look at the greetings in these opening verses. Philemon was evidently the host (so perhaps also the leader) of a house church. Paul writes to all the church members as well as to Philemon – addressing also Apphia, followed by Archippus.

Who was Apphia? Probably not Philemon's wife. When Paul writes 'the church in your house' (v. 2), the pronoun is singular – it is only Philemon's home. And when writing to other couples, such as Andronicus and Junia or Priscilla and Aquila, Paul addresses them jointly; he does not write to each as separate individuals, as he does to Apphia here. Moreover, the three people are described differently. The term 'sister' (v. 2), used to address Apphia, would usually designate a ministry colleague, just as Timothy is called 'brother' (v. 1).

Perhaps Apphia held a leadership role in this church; maybe she was a deacon like Phoebe. The letter leans heavily on Philemon to grant Onesimus freedom as well as forgiveness. Perhaps Paul felt he could count on Apphia's support.

What can this teach us? Among other things, to widen, not polarise, the discussion in contentious situations. Appealing to someone's better nature may meet with greater success if they think there are witnesses!

God of peace, give us wisdom in our dealings with one another.
Help us to be gentle, to persuade more than to argue or command.
And may we always choose to be kind. Amen

PENELOPE WILCOCK

Eunice and Lois of Lystra

I am reminded of your sincere faith, a faith that lived first in your grandmother Lois and your mother Eunice and now, I am sure, lives in you. For this reason I remind you to rekindle the gift of God that is within you through the laying on of my hands; for God did not give us a spirit of cowardice, but rather a spirit of power and of love and of self-discipline.

Civilisations the world over, throughout history, have tended towards male rulers. There are exceptions, but this is the norm. Usually, even when there is a woman at the head of government, the actual structures of government remain masculine in their nature. But even in countries where women are debarred from formal leadership, their sphere restricted to the home, they continue to be influential, shaping society.

We catch intriguing glimpses of this in the Bible. In the Old Testament, we see the strength of Jezebel putting backbone into Ahab (albeit not for good ends; 1 Kings 21:7) and Esther risking her life to speak up for her people. In the gospel of Luke, the first teaching we hear from Jesus (Luke 4:18–21) takes forward the themes of the song of Mary (Luke 1:46–55). Peter teaches that women should be gentle and submissive, but with a view to making change by subtle and quiet means (1 Peter 3:1–2).

Paul is in favour of preserving decorum and avoiding scandal, an advocate of winning the respect of our neighbours and sidestepping antagonism. Yet within the boundaries of tradition, he is open to women in leadership and respectful of their influence. In commending the sincerity of Timothy's faith, he acknowledges the influence of Timothy's mother and grandmother. He need not have done; many would have overlooked it, focusing only on the male leader. Paul is particular to notice and include the role of women.

In what ways has your family shaped your approach to life? In your faith, who has influenced you? What do you owe to quiet, unnoticed people?

Thank you, O God, for those whose gentle influence has spoken to me of your peace, those whose quiet, unassuming love showed me the power of your goodness. Amen

PENELOPE WILCOCK

The lady of 2 John

The elder to the elect lady and her children, whom I love in the truth, and not only I but also all who know the truth… I was overjoyed to find some of your children walking in the truth, just as we have been commanded by the Father. But now, dear lady, I ask you, not as though I were writing you a new commandment, but one we have had from the beginning, let us love one another.

Who was 'the lady' of 2 John? She is not only mysterious and nameless, but she has actually vanished altogether as a human person under the treatment of some New Testament scholars, who propose 'the lady and her children' to be the church and the members of its congregation.

Though in the New Testament, the word *kuria* (lady) occurs only in 2 John, we can find it elsewhere in literature of the ancient world, always referring to a high-status woman (sometimes the mistress of a household, or how a slave might address their owner). The term 'elect' or 'chosen', which has led some to believe this means the church itself, is also found elsewhere referring to human individuals – such as Paul's greeting to Rufus in Romans 16:13. John also refers to himself simply as 'the elder', which balances with 'the lady' aesthetically. Perhaps in times of persecution, personal identities were better kept discreet? The weight of evidence rests with 'the lady' being an individual recipient of the letter, not a church group.

An important lesson for us here is how easily people in minority groups can be dehumanised and made to disappear: those whose violent deaths are the 'collateral damage' of war; those who lead vulnerable and precarious lives of poverty, working in sweatshops so we can have cheap clothes. We will never learn how to love the ones whose existence we have not even noticed.

Father of all, help me look hard and ask questions. You who know the way through the valley of the shadow, help me see the people whose whole existence is lived in the shadows. You love them too. Amen

PENELOPE WILCOCK

Women and silence

I desire, then, that in every place the men should pray, lifting up holy hands without anger or argument... Let a woman learn in silence with full submission. I permit no woman to teach or to have authority over a man; she is to keep silent. For Adam was formed first, then Eve; and Adam was not deceived, but the woman was deceived and became a transgressor.

Towards the end of a fortnight looking at the New Testament's affirmation of women in leadership, we come to this passage about silenced women. How puzzling. I hold this text together in my mind with the similar teaching of 1 Corinthians 14:34–35, commanding women to keep silence in church, asking their husbands at home if they want to know anything.

What are we to make of this? How can we hold together the cultural progress we have made towards a world in which women may become visible equals with faithfulness to the Bible as our sacred text? Two suggestions.

First, the story of faith is not yet complete; our own lives continue to unfold the eternal gospel. The Bible, from Genesis to Revelation, tells of the people of God on a journey. Even in our glimpse of women in the New Testament, we see a progression, a paradox, in the way women are regarded. Given that outspoken and authoritative women leaders would have been culturally scandalous, perhaps we are looking at someone who went as far as he could for the context in which he had to work?

Second, though today we would not want to see women voiceless and oppressed, it is of course a sacred and beautiful thing to be a keeper of silence. Love and sorrow, faith and delight, powerful transformation, real understanding – these mostly happen in our silence.

Where does my life need silence? How can I use silence as an instrument of healing and love? Where have I heard the voice of God in the silence? What is the relationship between silence and peace?

O God, in silence I receive your love. In silence I submit to your healing wisdom. In silence I feel my way to peace. Amen

PENELOPE WILCOCK

Women and head covering

Just as woman came from man, so man comes through woman; but all things come from God. Judge for yourselves: is it proper for a woman to pray to God with her head unveiled? Does not nature itself teach you that if a man wears long hair, it is degrading to him, but if a woman has long hair, it is her glory? For her hair is given to her for a covering.

This passage comes from a large section in 1 Corinthians on the ordering of church life and public worship. Paul emphasises community, encouraging consideration for others and calm proceedings. Prophets are to take turns, not all shout out; tongues are to be interpreted; women are to participate quietly, not chat throughout or call across questions to their husbands; there is to be no grabbing big portions at the love feast. Church life is to be reverent, peaceful and loving.

This teaching on head covering is set in that context. It sounds odd at first; Paul seems to be saying both that the woman must wear a covering and that her hair is itself a covering. Which is it?

The answer probably lies in the Hippocratic understanding of male and female physiology, where hair of the head and body plays a significant role. In effect, a woman's hair was perceived as a sex organ comparable to the testicles of a man. In Hebrew law, attention is paid to ensuring genitalia are covered in worship – even for angels (see the euphemism of 'feet' in Isaiah 6:2). In the context of blended Greek and Hebrew cultural influences, Paul is ensuring that in the setting of public worship decency and modesty are observed. To achieve this in our own contemporary setting, we don't need to copy the recommended observance, but find our own authentic equivalent of appropriate modesty.

What expression of reverence and modesty is comfortable to you? Have you always felt this, or has your approach changed with evolving social attitudes or developing insights?

Holy God, in both worship and everyday life may we walk with reverence before you in every detail of our personal conduct. Amen

PENELOPE WILCOCK

Women and submission

Wives, be subject to your husbands as you are to the Lord. For the husband is the head of the wife just as Christ is the head of the church, the body of which he is the Saviour. Just as the church is subject to Christ, so also wives ought to be, in everything, to their husbands. Husbands, love your wives, just as Christ loved the church and gave himself up for her.

Ephesians 5 is, in my view, one of the most beautiful pieces of wisdom on personal relationships and marriage of all times. The teaching begins traditionally enough with the advice to wives to be subject to their husbands as to the Lord. One can imagine the men of the church nodding in approval as the letter is read out. Just as the church is subject to Christ, so a wife should submit to her husband.

It might have taken longer for the implications of the next part of the teaching to sink in: that, correspondingly, husbands must love and give themselves for their wives as Christ gave himself for the church. Wide open. Vulnerable. Nailed to a cross. Withholding nothing. Setting her free. That kind of love. To such a husband, any wife might cheerfully submit; such a marriage would always offer security but never deteriorate into bondage.

This teaching is deeper and wiser than 'do your own thing'. Paul accepts the situation of male dominance that proceeds from the fall, but gives it back to us redeemed by the salvation offered in Christ – the Lord who walked among us as one who serves.

What do you think will make a happy marriage? How much of male or female nature is biological and how much cultural? What do you think 'submission' means? How should a person both cultivate a gentle servant heart and protect herself or himself against abuse?

In your own image you made us male and female, mysterious God.
You understand our nature because all reality proceeds from you.
You are our creator. May our lives in their small way express your creative
power, your holiness, your wonder, your endless variety and your
unconditional love. Amen

PENELOPE WILCOCK

The presence of God

I am involved with the ministry of healing, and a subject that seems to come to the fore more and more is that of the presence of God. If there is one thing that differentiates Christian healing from any other form of therapy, it is the fact that it is centred around the person of Jesus – the essence of the presence of God. Yet this is not just true of healing. The presence of God is something that touches upon our worship, our prayer lives and our very existence.

The presence of God is an evocative phrase that may mean something different for each of us. It might suggest a holy place where God is perceived to dwell in a particularly powerful way: a 'thin place' where the boundary between heaven and earth seems blurred. This could be a local church, a grand cathedral, an ancient shrine or any other holy spot. At times we may hear of people flocking to such a place if God's presence is reported to be there.

Others would describe the presence of God more as an awareness of his closeness that comes over us. It is like a feeling that cannot be manufactured or produced for ourselves but just seems to happen, often at quite unexpected times. It is rather like our natural world being invaded with a new consciousness of God.

The presence of God is also something that we seek at certain key moments of our lives, often when a weighty decision needs to be made or a specific need arises. Yet at times like this, sadly it is a sense of his absence, rather than his presence, that is more commonly found.

So, what is the presence of God? Is it really about atmosphere and feelings, or could it be something different – a profound truth for us to grasp, take seriously and allow to change and transform our lives?

Over the next two weeks, we will be looking at some accounts of the presence of God that are recorded in the Bible, and thinking about what we can learn from them that is relevant for our own lives.

JOHN RYELAND

God's presence is everywhere

Where can I go from your Spirit? Where can I flee from your presence? If I go up to the heavens, you are there; if I make my bed in the depths, you are there.

It can be tempting to think that if we don't actively seek the presence of God, we are in danger of missing it altogether. While it is certainly true that most of us are aware of his presence to a greater or lesser extent at various times, this psalm reminds us that God's presence is constant, whether or not we have an awareness of him.

Having said that, it is probably our being aware of his presence that makes all the difference. If we could sense the presence of Jesus with us, it is likely that we would find a new significance to our prayer lives and a fresh confidence in our attempts to share the good news with others. However, the flip side is that if we don't feel God's presence, it is easy to assume that he is not there as much as at other times – or is even absent altogether. Yet today's psalm assures us that the presence of God is so real that it is impossible to flee from him.

Other Bible passages also speak about the constancy of God's presence, such as the final words in Matthew's gospel: 'And surely I am with you always, to the very end of the age' (Matthew 28:20). The wonderful promise is that, regardless of whether or not we feel it, Jesus is always with us.

In so many areas – the presence of God included – truth and feelings should not be confused. You are in the very presence of God right now, whatever your situation and no matter what you are feeling, and an appropriate response is to pause and ponder the implications of this glorious truth. Right now, you are with God and he is with you.

Close your eyes, take a few deep breaths and, before you begin to express or verbalise anything in prayer, recognise the truth that you are in God's presence. He is with you, he knows everything about you, he loves you deeply – and he will never go away.

JOHN RYELAND

Being unaware of God's presence

Jesus himself came up and walked along with them; but they were kept from recognising him.

There is something reassuring about the fact that, as these two disciples walked along the road towards the village of Emmaus, the physical presence of the risen Lord Jesus was only a few feet away from them and yet they missed it completely. They had no idea it was him! How comforting for us, because there are probably countless times each day when we too are totally unaware that God himself is with us.

We are not told what it was that prevented the two on the Emmaus road from recognising Jesus – possibly their own incredulity, grief and confusion about recent events, or even the hand of God. Whatever it was, we as onlookers have a clearer perception of what was going on than the travellers themselves. We can sympathise with them, as at times our own lives can feel equally confusing and we struggle to understand what is happening, why people behave as they do, how things can go so wrong and why we don't see answers to our prayers.

However, despite their emotions, questions and total confusion, Jesus was with those travellers on the road – even though they didn't realise it at first. Likewise, he is also with us in our own uncertainty about many aspects of life, so let's try to recognise his presence with each of us.

Yesterday we were reminded that the presence of God is constantly with us. It is not a reward for right thinking and faithful service but is a reality for all of us to cling to, even in the darkest and most confusing of times. In the presence of Jesus, those two travellers were encouraged to be honest about what they were feeling and why – and so are we!

However you are feeling right now, and despite anything that suggests otherwise, hold on to the truth that Jesus is by your side. Once you have acknowledged this, talk to him about what is on your mind, knowing that he is listening intently to you as he walks with you along life's path.

JOHN RYELAND

Jesus reveals the Father's heart

Philip said, 'Lord, show us the Father and that will be enough for us.' Jesus answered: 'Don't you know me, Philip, even after I have been among you such a long time? Anyone who has seen me has seen the Father... Don't you believe that I am in the Father, and that the Father is in me?'

I wonder if there is a touch of despair in the voice of Jesus as he answers Philip's question. He may well have hoped that Philip would have understood by now that all his ministry had been about revealing the Father to us.

Jesus was saying that all his wonderful words and actions were reflections of his Father. When he went about teaching and doing good, it was the Father's heart that he was mirroring; as he spoke about forgiveness, it was his Father's desire for forgiveness he was proclaiming; when he healed the sick, he was demonstrating his Father's heart to heal.

He took this to a whole new level when he said, 'This, then, is how you should pray: "Our Father in heaven"' (Matthew 6:9). In other words, Jesus wants us to begin our prayers by focusing on the truth that we have a heavenly Father and that we are his dearly loved children. This close identity between Jesus and his Father reveals this truth that we all have a perfect father-like presence with us in our lives, whatever our own experience of fatherhood might be.

Jesus was pointing out that as we grasp the reality of the presence of God in our lives, it encompasses far more than a relationship with him – the healing, active and sacrificial Jesus. We are also privileged to experience the abiding presence of one who stands with us and fathers us throughout the amazing joys, perplexing moments and sometimes deep pits that make up our lives.

When you ponder the presence of God with you, what is he like? What is your expectation of him? What is your reaction to him? How does this compare with what Jesus was seeking to reveal to us?

JOHN RYELAND

Why does God give us his presence?

'I have come that they may have life, and have it to the full.'

The presence of God is a constant reality for us; regardless of whether or not we are aware of him, he is here! So what can we hope for as a result of his presence? We have a clue to this from today's bold statement that Jesus made about the reason for his incarnation: he came so that we might have abundant life.

If you look at the context for this statement, it appears that Jesus was standing next to the man whose eyesight he had previously restored. After the Pharisees had interrogated the man about his healing, he had been thrown out of the synagogue, but Jesus tracked him down and it is at this point that he addressed the Pharisees – and no doubt others who had gathered around – to speak about his desire to bring people abundant life. No doubt the man who had been born blind appreciated his new-found abundant life through his miraculous healing, but what this new life looks like will be different for each of us.

I like to think of abundant life, or healing, as us becoming the people we were created to be. This is why Jesus came to our world, and his constant presence with us today is still seeking this.

His presence can be wonderfully comforting and encouraging, but he wants more than this. Regardless of whether or not we are aware of his presence, he is seeking to transform us in every way – our bodies, attitudes, prejudices and reactions to others.

There is nothing selfish about seeking the presence of God. In fact, if his presence transforms us it is one of the most powerful things we can ever seek and, for the sake of those with whom we come into contact, one of the most needed.

God has promised that he will always be with you, so as you sit in his presence invite him to touch you with his transforming touch. You may have your own agenda of how you would like to be transformed, but give him permission to change you according to his agenda.

JOHN RYELAND

The presence of Jesus leads to healing

And the people all tried to touch him, because power was coming from him and healing them all.

This verse says something stunning about the presence of God in Jesus – that he was a source of healing. The Bible presents us with different pictures of the healing ministry of Jesus. It seems that sometimes he searched out those in need of healing and other times he responded to those who sought him out. On this occasion, however, he seemed to be like an open fountain, with healing flowing to all who touched him. What's more, it seems that it did not matter who came to him, what they were suffering from, how good they had been or even what the attitude of their hearts was. The people sought to touch him because healing was flowing from him.

The implication of this for us is obvious – our transformation is not first and foremost about us and what we do, but rather about our connection with the presence of God.

This verse does not tell us the details of how people were healed – if they were healed in the way they wanted or whether Jesus spoke to them and, if he did, what he said or asked – but certainly as they connected with his presence something happened.

We are all in need of transformation, whether we long for it or are unaware of our need, and it begins when we actively connect with the presence of God. This does not mean that he won't involve others in the process, such as seeking advice from medical professionals or the wisdom of friends, but our transformation begins with us turning to God as the initial source of all that we need.

As you begin to pray, before you bring anything to God, trust in the reality of his presence with you. Don't rush on. Slowly and honestly bring yourself to him – the parts of you that have much to be thankful for, as well as those parts that you might rather hide away. They are all part of you with whom he longs to connect.

JOHN RYELAND

It's all about connecting with God's presence

'If I just touch his clothes, I will be healed.'

The story of the woman who touched the clothes of Jesus is a beautiful and powerful account of connecting with the presence of God. Interestingly, her action interrupted another healing story, that of Jairus' daughter.

In some ways the whole story is quite disturbing. Jesus was on his way to minister to a dying girl – by anyone's standards something of a priority – when this woman interrupted him on his journey. Even worse, she reached out to touch him, which potentially rendered him unclean and restricted his ministry to others. However, not only did Jesus stop and respond to her, but he actually commended her for her faith!

This suggests to me that it is always appropriate to try to connect with Jesus. You may feel that it is not the right time, that Jesus has other priorities or that there are others in more need than you, but none of this mattered to the woman in the story who was commended by Jesus. Perhaps we, too, should not let such concerns worry us.

Since the presence of God is sacred, it can be tempting to believe that it is too holy for us. We may feel very ordinary in comparison to others, and suspect that we are not the kind of people who are ever likely to draw close to the presence of God – let alone receive his transforming touch. This story suggests otherwise. It reveals that Jesus longs for people to connect with him and to experience the good things that flow from him. We should never feel that it is inappropriate for us to reach out to him.

Be honest about your own situation. How do you feel you compare with other people? Do you believe that Jesus would actually want to be with you?

Now follow that honesty with the truth of how Jesus is revealed in the Bible. He loved to share his presence with those who were sick, with sinners and with the people the world looked down upon.

---

*Hold your honesty about yourself up to the truth about him
and call out to him with confidence.*

JOHN RYELAND

Jesus didn't go away

He who descended is the very one who ascended higher than all the heavens, in order to fill the whole universe.

Traditional pictures of the ascension present us with an image of Jesus physically rising to heaven – a departure or going away. Nothing could be further from the truth! According to Matthew 28:20, the words Jesus spoke at this time were far from a goodbye and instead signified more of his presence: 'And surely I am with you always, to the very end of the age.'

Today's verse from Ephesians takes such thinking about the ascension even further. Again, far from signifying a departure, Jesus' ascension is about filling the whole universe. This seems impossible to get our heads around, but the sense is that whereas Christ filled a human body during his earthly ministry, now his presence fills the universe. A similar thought is expressed in Ephesians 1:23, where the author writes of Christ as one 'who fills everything in every way'.

This takes the idea of the presence of God with us to a whole new level. It is not just about God being with us, but about Christ filling the whole universe. So rather than him joining us in our lives, it is about us being part of a Christ-filled universe – we cannot go anywhere he is not. Having said this, we are still encouraged to 'be filled with the Spirit' (Ephesians 5:18), as there is a sense in which we must appropriate for ourselves what is already there.

As with so much about the presence of God, it comes down to our reliance (or not) on our feelings. It is unlikely that we 'feel' the presence of Christ filling the universe, which is presumably why scripture reveals it to us. But now it has been revealed, the challenge for us is to grow in our wonder of it.

Take a moment to sit quietly for a few moments. Begin by whispering the name of 'Jesus' to remind yourself of his presence with you. Then repeat this truth to yourself several times, 'You fill everything in every way,' perhaps using it in time with your breathing.

JOHN RYELAND

The transforming power of God's presence (1)

As he neared Damascus on his journey, suddenly a light from heaven flashed around him. He fell to the ground and heard a voice say to him, 'Saul, Saul, why do you persecute me?'

The conversion of Saul is certainly one of the most dramatic stories of the New Testament. It encapsulates the moment when a man charged with destroying the Christian church had a total change of heart and began his journey towards becoming its chief evangelist. It was his dramatic encounter with the presence of God that brought about the change in him. His encounter was so profound and physical that it changed his whole perception of the nature of God and the course of his own life.

Is there anything that we can learn from Saul's encounter, given that it was entirely engineered by God and not based on human initiative? I suspect that very few of us have had an experience like Saul's – and indeed this seems to have been a one-off incident for him. Yet what it points to is the personal nature of experiencing the presence of God.

It appears that the apostle Paul never questioned the authenticity of people's faith because their experiences had not been similar to his, and yet we can be so quick to judge. We find it easy to assume that others ought to share our experiences or beliefs, or we judge our own experiences to be of a different or lesser nature from those of other people and find ourselves wanting as a result.

We may honour the religious experiences in our lives or choose to play them down because they do not seem as powerful as the experiences others have. However, these moments are God's gift to us.

As you look back over your life, what have been some of the moments you would describe as religious experiences, or times when you were particularly aware of God's presence? How would you describe those moments? Can you recall any events in your life leading up to those times? What was their effect on you?

JOHN RYELAND

The transforming power of God's presence (2)

'Zacchaeus, come down immediately. I must stay at your house today.'

Yesterday we began to think about moments of religious experience in our lives. We also touched on the futility of comparing our experiences with those of others. Perhaps it is not the nature of the experience that really matters, but what we do as a result and how we let it shape us.

The story of Zacchaeus is a powerful account of a person encountering the presence of God. It is light years away from the dramatic nature of Saul's encounter with Jesus, which we considered yesterday – no bright lights, falling down or being struck blind – but it is an equally powerful story of a person allowing their encounter with the presence of God to transform them.

It is unclear from the text how much time Jesus spent with Zacchaeus, but at the end of the encounter Zacchaeus was willing to pay back those he had cheated, and his heart was evidently changed as a new wave of generosity came over him. The effect of his transformation must have been staggering for those who witnessed it.

No doubt there were many people who had encounters with Jesus in those days, either listening to him teach or being healed by him, but we seldom hear about the effect of this upon them. As we recall some of our own encounters with Jesus, those moments of religious experience, what have we done with them? However dramatic or small we may judge them to be, the challenge is how we let them change us. For this reason, perhaps some of the most challenging encounters with God are not the dramatic moments but the smaller ones, because they are easy to miss or ignore. Yet, taken seriously, they can be moments of real change for us.

Think back over some of the main religious experiences of your life. What was the effect of them at the time? Did they produce change in your lifestyle, beliefs or attitudes? As you reflect upon them again, what has been their long-term effect?

JOHN RYELAND

God's presence can be threatening

Going on from that place, he went into their synagogue, and a man with a shrivelled hand was there. Looking for a reason to bring charges against Jesus, they asked him, 'Is it lawful to heal on the Sabbath?'

There is something very dramatic about this passage. Some Pharisees were standing close to Jesus, the incarnate presence of God, plotting how they could bring charges against him, and by the end of this healing story they had decided to kill him. They were totally unsettled by Jesus and by the threat they perceived him to be to their way of life and religion. There is a saying that God offends the mind to reveal the heart; perhaps there is a message in this for us too.

Why does God seem to be particularly present at certain times but not at others? Why is it that some people seem to have an increased sense of his presence? Why does the presence of God not lead to greater things in our lives? These are all good questions, but they probably don't have answers that will satisfy us. If we are brave, however, we can allow the questions to reveal something about our hearts. Are we resentful or envious of other people's experiences of God? Are we disappointed in our own experience of his presence?

Of course, the value of reflecting on such questions depends on our willingness to be honest with ourselves. Honest answers can be so revealing and lead to any number of positive steps: a time of reflection, hunger for more of God's presence, repentance of the way we view others or a deeper appreciation of what we do have. A lack of honesty, however, may begin to creep in if we find ourselves putting up masks so that other people don't glimpse our uncertainties about God. Perhaps it is only by facing up to our feelings that we are able to grow through them.

Spend a few minutes reflecting honestly on your own experience of the presence of God. Are you envious of the way other people seem to experience him? Are you dissatisfied with the nature of your own experience of God? What will you do with the answers to these questions?

JOHN RYELAND

What will we do with God's presence?

So Judas came to the garden, guiding a detachment of soldiers and some officials from the chief priests and the Pharisees. They were carrying torches, lanterns and weapons. Jesus, knowing all that was going to happen to him, went out and asked them, 'Who is it you want?' 'Jesus of Nazareth,' they replied. 'I am he,' Jesus said. (And Judas the traitor was standing there with them.) When Jesus said, 'I am he,' they drew back and fell to the ground.

When the soldiers came to arrest Jesus, they were overwhelmed by the presence of God and fell to the ground. The catalyst for this seems to be Jesus saying, 'I am he.' This was not just a simple matter of Jesus confirming his identity, but a revelation of him as the great 'I am' – the very presence of God. At that moment of revelation, the soldiers (who probably had no idea of the significance of the words he had just spoken) fell to the ground.

I wonder what they said to each other upon regaining their composure. Were they wondering what had just happened to them and why they all spontaneously fell to the ground? Did they talk about it later? It seems from the text that the experience had little effect on them, apart from the fact that they fell over. This is interesting as we ponder our own awareness of the presence of God.

In the New Testament, we read of others who came to acknowledge the uniqueness of Jesus seemingly without any particular personal experience – Nicodemus (John 3:2) and a centurion (Matthew 8:8–9). In other words, it is not simply the experience of the presence of God that we need to change us, but a dwelling on the person of Jesus as revealed to us in the Bible.

Perhaps what we need to ponder is what our faith is built upon.

Are your experiences of God's presence foundational to what you believe? Do you wish you could have had more? Have you been unable to make sense of some experiences?

JOHN RYELAND

How does God see us?

'Now my eyes will be open and my ears attentive to the prayers offered in this place. I have chosen and consecrated this temple so that my Name may be there for ever. My eyes and my heart will always be there.'

This passage concerns the building of the temple, but it contains something wonderful for us. When Solomon constructed the temple, he dedicated it to God and expressed his desire for what the temple would come to mean for his subjects. That night, God appeared to Solomon and gave him his vision for his temple – that it would be a place of his presence, so that coming to the temple would be as if one were coming to the very presence of God.

The way in which the presence of God is described is so personal. It is not simply something like a cloud hovering over the people, but it is about an intense attentiveness to them, watching over them and his heart dwelling with them.

There are implications in this for us since Paul wrote, 'Do you not know that your bodies are temples of the Holy Spirit?' (1 Corinthians 6:19), which we will return to on Saturday. If we are to take seriously our status as temples of the Holy Spirit, we need to recognise God's acute attentiveness to us and his heart for us, not only as a body gathered together, but as unique individuals as well.

It is tempting to think of God noting all our sins and failings, but the good news is that his loving watchfulness sees every part of us, including the good things we do, the secret acts of kindness and the times our hearts are broken. He sees it all.

Take these words from 2 Chronicles, and instead of applying them to a physical building, apply them to yourself: 'Father, your eyes are open, and your ears attentive to my prayers. You have chosen and consecrated me so that your Name may be in me. Your eyes and your heart are always with me.' Whisper this prayer and catch his delight in you.

JOHN RYELAND

No such thing as a trouble-free life

I bear your name, Lord God Almighty.

This verse brings home both the simplicity and profundity of our relationship with God – we carry his presence with us wherever we go. It is interesting that although Jeremiah was aware that he carried the presence of God, this certainly did not mean that he led a charmed and trouble-free life. Just reading chapter 15, where this verse is found, allows us to glimpse a suffering man. Jeremiah saw himself as cursed by others, persecuted, suffering reproach, pained and wounded. He would certainly not have described his life as a bed of roses!

So if we are touched by God and truly bear his presence, why don't things go more smoothly for us? If you have ever thought this, you are certainly not alone. One of the most comforting lessons we can learn is that hardship does not mean that God has abandoned us, nor that he is displeased and punishing us. When we find ourselves going through hard times, it can be tempting to assume that we are at fault, to take it personally and to allow it to shape our opinion of ourselves. However, this was not true of Jeremiah, and it is not true for us.

It is so easy to think negatively, but the antidote to this is to remind ourselves of the reality of God's presence with us. I have always found the seven words in today's verse a great help to carry with me throughout the day. Sometimes I try to link my pattern of breathing to them: as I breathe in I focus on the words 'I bear your name', and as I breathe out, 'Lord God Almighty'. When I have done this for a few minutes in the morning, I often find myself coming back to this phrase throughout the day and finding comfort in its truth. We can do this whatever our circumstances, whether we need grace and reassurance or simply a reminder of God's constant presence with us.

Try the meditation mentioned above. Breathe in, and focus on the words 'I bear your name'. Breathe out, and focus on 'Lord God Almighty'.

JOHN RYELAND

Being a temple of the Holy Spirit

Do you not know that your bodies are temples of the Holy Spirit, who is in you, whom you have received from God?

The context of this verse is Paul encouraging people to flee from sexual immorality and to see their bodies as God sees them – temples of the Holy Spirit. There are a few lessons here as we conclude our studies looking at the wonder of the presence of God.

First, Paul's teaching applies to all of us. He wrote to the whole church rather than specific members, and his letter reveals that the church in Corinth was far from perfect in many ways. We may feel unworthy to be temples of the Holy Spirit – but that is not the point. Being a temple is not a reward for our goodness or holiness; it describes what we are, and we need to work out the implications of this.

Second, being a temple of the Holy Spirit is not our idea. It is God who has decided that this is the case, and he has done what it takes for it to happen.

Finally, this is what we were created to be. It strikes me that temples are designed specifically to be temples. It is unlikely that any builder would start work on a new building and decide half-way through what it could be used for. Instead he would have the plans for the building and create it accordingly. In the same way, God has planned, designed and created us to be temples of his Holy Spirit. This is what he sees when he looks at us, and this is what it is natural for us to be.

You may not understand why God has created you to be a temple. You may be a good or bad temple, but you cannot escape the truth of what you are – a dwelling place for his presence.

You are a temple of the Holy Spirit. How does this make you feel? What difference will you let it make to you in the hours and days ahead?

JOHN RYELAND

Harvest

As a young person in England, I remember lavish harvest festivals and the harvest suppers that followed, where I was induced to sample the doubtful delicacy of pumpkin pie – it has taken the wide variety of pumpkins we enjoy in New Zealand to re-educate my taste! Harvest festivals seem to have gone out of fashion here; I hope you are still enjoying them in the northern hemisphere.

Harvest happens continuously all over the planet. I'm writing this in the southern spring, where we are seeing a harvest of new lambs, while those in the north are celebrating the harvesting of crops. Every time we sit down to a meal and give thanks for the food, we are celebrating a mini harvest festival.

The need to recognise God as creator of 'seedtime and harvest' (Genesis 8:22, NIV) is universal. It is a recurrent Old Testament theme, and the New Testament tends to use harvest as a metaphor for a number of things, such as events, actions and rewards. Just check how many of Jesus' parables have harvest themes! One of our old harvest thanksgiving hymns – Henry Alford's 'Come, ye thankful people, come' – has a powerful reference to Jesus' parable of the weeds (Matthew 13:36–43):

> *All this world is God's own field, fruit unto his praise to yield;*
> *Wheat and tares together sown, unto joy or sorrow grown.*

The season of Advent is on the horizon. This is the time in the church calendar when our thoughts are directed towards Jesus' second coming. The Bible speaks of this in several places as being the ultimate harvest, in either an individual or a global sense.

During this coming fortnight, we will be looking at harvest references throughout the Bible and will find that harvest is given a number of different meanings by the biblical writers. What is the first thing that comes to mind now as you think of harvest? Is it just the physical human activity of gathering in the crops? I wonder if that will have changed by the time we have finished these reflections together.

PAUL GRAVELLE

Harvest gifts

Abel became a shepherd, but Cain was a farmer. After some time Cain brought some of his harvest and gave it as an offering to the Lord. Then Abel brought the first lamb born to one of his sheep, killed it, and gave the best parts of it as an offering. The Lord was pleased with Abel and his offering, but he rejected Cain and his offering. Cain became furious, and he scowled in anger.

Harvest festivals in church can sometimes feature unbecoming little rivalries. Who arranges the best fruit basket, grows the biggest cabbage, bakes the crustiest loaf? In Genesis 4 we have the first account of a harvest festival. Not a very lavish one, you might say – only two offerings – but the rivalry was there just the same and in this case with a tragic result. We may be puzzled by God's rejection of Cain's offering. Was there some hidden reason that made sheep-meat somehow more acceptable than grain, or was it something else?

Paul, writing to the Corinthian Christians about charitable giving, tells us that 'God loves the one who gives gladly' (2 Corinthians 9:7). Cain seems to have been a quick-tempered person, probably prone to unreasoned jealousy. God didn't just reject Cain's harvest gift out of hand; it seems that he first rejected Cain's attitude in giving.

There was something else about Abel's gift that we should note, because that too could have provoked Cain's anger. Abel was careful to present only the best parts of the lamb he had killed. Is there a hint that Cain had been too casual in selecting the quality of grain he was offering? Whatever we present to God should always be the very best that we can offer, whether it is wealth, work, worship or anything else.

A casual attitude in our offering positions us uncomfortably close to Cain. God has given us himself. Whatever we offer to him, in church, at home or wherever, let it be only the very best.

Self-giving God, I am not always a cheerful giver; my sense of duty sometimes gets in the way. Help me in my efforts to give of my best.

PAUL GRAVELLE

Festival regulations

Each family is to bring two loaves of bread and present them to the Lord as a special gift... And with the bread the community is to present seven one-year-old lambs, one bull, and two rams, none of which may have any defects. They shall be offered as a burnt offering to the Lord, along with a grain offering and a wine offering... Your descendants are to observe this regulation for all time to come.

For the Jewish people in Old Testament times, keeping to the regulations in the law of Moses was their prime means of relating to God and indeed formed their identity as God's chosen people. Those of us who are accustomed to free-form worship will be horrified at the thought of being regulated to that degree. Those of us who are used to a more liturgical order in church may need to check that we are not letting the rites obscure the reason we are there.

When Jesus arrived on the scene, he encountered a culture in which the regulations found in Exodus, Leviticus, Numbers and Deuteronomy were interpreted out of all proportion and in such minute detail as to be almost laughable. Fulfilling the spirit of the law, rather than adding to its detail, was the subject of Jesus' most vehement sermons! Could we, I wonder, be erring in the other direction? Harvest festival celebrations are now something of a rare event here in New Zealand. I suspect that saying grace at mealtimes may also be a disappearing ritual – we will be talking about that in a couple of days.

Running through the five books of Moses, we can find a number of regulations that clearly safeguard health and well-being. These were designed particularly for a tribe wandering in the desert. However, the regular recognition of God as the provider of our daily food and giving him thanks, by means of harvest festivals, crop blessings and saying grace, are certainly not things we should set aside from either the calendar or our routine in our more purpose-filled days.

Lord God, without your provision we would have no food;
without your love we would have no life; without your sacrifice
we would have no hope. Amen

PAUL GRAVELLE

Remember the poor

'When you harvest your fields, do not cut the grain at the edges of the fields, and do not go back to cut the heads of grain that were left. Do not go back through your vineyard to gather the grapes that were missed or to pick up the grapes that have fallen; leave them for poor people and foreigners. I am the Lord your God.'

The instruction about grain-harvesting is repeated later in Leviticus (see 23:22), but the one about fruit-picking has a particular application for us in New Zealand, where fruit is beginning to take over from sheep as the primary industry. The provision in Leviticus is, of course, part of God's concern for the disadvantaged and the setting-up of a simple form of social security for those who could not provide for themselves – widows, orphans and others similarly impoverished.

Fruit harvest time here means that there are never enough local workers to pick the crop. In the Pacific Islands, there are many able-bodied folk without adequate work to sustain their families, and hundreds of these are granted short-term work visas every year to help with gathering, sorting and packing the fruit. In addition to their wages, I believe that the fruit-pickers also receive practical benefits not unlike those accorded to the poor in Old Testament days.

Is this passage just about remembering the poor? Yes and no. You may recall the story of Ruth, in which Boaz goes over the top and instructs his harvest workers to let Ruth take virtually all the grain she needs, even from sheaves already harvested. Boaz has heard about Ruth's virtuous loyalty to Naomi and discerns her to be deserving.

If you are like me, you may sometimes hesitate to give money to beggars on the street, wondering if they are feeding an addiction, rather than an empty stomach. The growing number of homeless people on our city streets presents problems of both conscience and logistics. But scripture doesn't seem to make any distinction in terms of worthiness when it comes to the poor. It simply says, 'Give.'

'I have no money at all, but I give you what I have: in the name of Jesus Christ of Nazareth…' (Acts 3:6).

PAUL GRAVELLE

Daily bread

You show your care for the land by sending rain; you make it rich and fertile. You fill the streams with water; you provide the earth with crops. This is how you do it: you send abundant rain on the ploughed fields and soak them with water; you soften the soil with showers and cause the young plants to grow. What a rich harvest your goodness provides!

Grace at mealtimes, thanksgiving for the food, has always been a practice in our family – even in restaurants, to the embarrassment of some of the younger ones! We pray, 'Give us today our daily bread,' as one of the earliest petitions in the Lord's Prayer, so it seems a good idea to give thanks for our food regularly, particularly as harvest festivals seem to be going out of fashion. After all, a once-a-year thanksgiving seems a bit inadequate for a three-times-daily provision, doesn't it?

In several regions of the world, harvests are inadequate and people face hardship as a result. At times this is the result of changes in the weather pattern or other natural disasters that cause crops to fail, but often it is because of the unthinking and careless commercial or industrial activity of others. There are individuals and organisations who, by putting their own interests first, without due consideration of the effects, are affecting both the lives of others and the balance of the natural environment. We need to remember that creation was crafted perfectly in the beginning and that even the natural disasters, which seem to be happening so frequently these days, are ultimately the consequence of humanity's wrong choices.

'Make us mindful of the needs of others,' is said as part of a mealtime grace that many use. Harvest thanksgivings used to involve distributing the produce on display to the needy. What might we be doing to help alleviate the plight of those who are hungry in our world today?

We receive this food in gratitude to God and to all who have helped to bring it to our table. Help us to respond to those in need with wisdom and compassion. Amen

PAUL GRAVELLE

Sowing and reaping

'Take a good look at the fields; the crops are now ripe and ready to be harvested! The one who reaps the harvest is being paid and gathers the crops for eternal life; so the one who plants and the one who reaps will be glad together. For the saying is true, "Someone plants, someone else reaps." I have sent you to reap a harvest in a field where you did not work.'

The Samaritan woman whom Jesus spoke with at the well has gone off to collect her townsfolk. The disciples arrive and, among other things, are concerned that he needs food but, as so often, Jesus turns his answer into a teaching parable of the kingdom. He sees the patriarchs and prophets of the Old Testament as sowers. Now, here are the twelve, designated to work with him as reapers, gathering the human harvest into eternal life.

In 1911 George Steven wrote, 'There have been long periods of the church's history when there were no revivals and no Christian work but that of the steady teaching and preaching of the truth and the influence of Christian personalities.' There is no dispute about the need for sowers to be at work in anticipation of the reapers. In these studies, however, we are concentrating on the harvest and, like the disciples, we are all called to some aspect of the work of harvesting the crops for eternal life.

In earlier days, harvest time would involve virtually everyone in the community in some role or other. Crops had to be cut or lifted, bound in sheaves or otherwise gathered, and threshed or prepared for storage. Workers in the field had to be fed, animals cared for and so on. Everyone in the village would have a task until harvest was safely 'home'.

Not all of us are evangelists, perhaps, but every one of us has a role to play in bringing the harvest of the lost into the eternal life of the kingdom of God. Nothing is more important than this.

How can I best help in the vital work of bringing the harvest home to eternal life?

PAUL GRAVELLE

Wheat and weeds – the parable

'A man sowed good seed in his field. One night... an enemy came and sowed weeds among the wheat and went away... The man's servants came to him and said, "Sir, it was good seed you sowed in your field; where did the weeds come from?... Do you want us to go and pull up the weeds?"... "No," he answered, "... Let the wheat and weeds both grow together until harvest."'

Speaking to people familiar with sowing and reaping, it is little wonder that so many of Jesus' parables touch on aspects of harvest. Tomorrow we will have a look at Jesus' explanation of this story; today let's look at a problem that seems to concern a lot of people: why does God allow terrible things to happen? How can good and evil exist side by side? Why can't the weeds simply be pulled up?

We are all too aware of the sin-polluted nature of the world we live in. Daily newscasts remind us of that. And the cause is inescapable, though the fact seems to be ignored by many complainants; it is brought about by the wrong choices we humans have been making ever since Adam and Eve. We are guilty of allowing the enemy to get in and sow the weeds!

However, no parable covers every aspect of the situation it portrays. While we cannot root out the weeds themselves, there are things we can do to stop them from spreading. Many of God's people are actively engaged in preventing the spread of ignorance, poverty, disease, violence, crime, homelessness and other expressions of evil. Many more are supporting them through prayer, finance, messages of encouragement and other means.

But the uncomfortable truth is that the weeds in the parable actually represent people – those who, for one reason or another, persist in ignoring God's purpose for their lives. The great commission at the end of Matthew's gospel is about changing people; Jesus says, 'Go, then, to all peoples everywhere and make them my disciples' (Matthew 28:19), or, 'Go and turn the weeds into wheat!'

Lord, help me to play my part in turning weeds into wheat
for your kingdom.

PAUL GRAVELLE

Wheat and weeds – the explanation

His disciples came to him and said, 'Tell us what the parable about the weeds in the field means.' Jesus answered, 'The man who sowed the good seed is the Son of Man; the field is the world; the good seed is the people who belong to the Kingdom; the weeds are the people who belong to the Evil One; and the enemy who sowed the weeds is the Devil. The harvest is the end of the age, and the harvest workers are angels. Just as the weeds are gathered up and burned in the fire, so the same thing will happen at the end of the age.'

Hellfire and damnation are not popular sermon topics today. In his explanation of the parable of the weeds, however, Jesus doesn't hesitate to state it as he sees it. Speaking with those close to him, Jesus doesn't pull any punches. He gets quite explicit about the ultimate fate of the perpetrators of evil! Whatever the ultimate outcome of these words from Jesus' lips, this is not the only parable in which he uses harvest as a metaphor for a future time of reckoning.

Unless there is some imminent threat of nuclear annihilation, we seldom give much thought to the prospect of the 'end of the age' (v. 39). While we should certainly not become obsessed with the future, it is equally dangerous to ignore the matter altogether. Jesus clearly thought his disciples needed to know what to expect and took pains to answer their question in considerable detail. Matthew devotes two whole chapters (24 and 25) to it!

Whenever Jesus speaks about his kingdom and that of the evil one, he never mentions a neutral position between them. You would probably not be reading this if you were an avowed member of the latter! But it would be good for us all to reaffirm our loyalty to the kingdom of the risen Lord Jesus Christ.

Lord God, I hereby affirm my loyal adherence to the kingdom of your Son, the risen Lord Jesus Christ, prince of peace and lord of lords. Amen

PAUL GRAVELLE

Harvest workers

As he saw the crowds, his heart was filled with pity for them, because they were worried and helpless, like sheep without a shepherd. So he said to his disciples, 'The harvest is large, but there are few workers to gather it in. Pray to the owner of the harvest that he will send out workers to gather in his harvest.'

Our experience of sheep here in New Zealand is that they only appear worried and helpless when the shepherds muster them in for shearing, drenching or trucking to the freezing works. Things must have been different for sheep in Matthew's day.

The disciples faced a huge task and, even though Jesus later reinforced their efforts with a supplementary force of 72, it was not until after the empowering of the Holy Spirit that thousands of converts began to be gathered.

Jesus sees the harvest as people, but the harvest workers also are human, rather than angelic. He expresses concern that the weeds will not become wheat before gathering time arrives, but implies that transformation is possible. Moses put it starkly to the people before they entered the promised land when he said, 'I am now giving you the choice between… God's blessing and God's curse, and I call heaven and earth to witness the choice you make. Choose life' (Deuteronomy 30:19). Everyone has the choice, but there is an ever-present need for those who have already made the choice to be 'wheat' in the kingdom of God to become active workers in one of the many capacities that are possible and available.

Jesus calls all of us who identify as his disciples to pray for more harvest workers. We are surrounded, every day, by people who are 'planting in the field of their natural desires' (Galatians 6:8) and who are not aware of the danger this involves. There are never enough who are willing to help such people.

Lord, God of the harvest, your Son asks us to pray for more workers to spread the good news of eternal life. By your Spirit, show us what we can do to help bring this about and keep us ever aware of the need. Amen

PAUL GRAVELLE

A harvest of eternal life

You will reap exactly what you plant. If you plant in the field of your natural desires, from it you will gather the harvest of death; if you plant in the field of the Spirit, from the Spirit you will gather the harvest of eternal life. So let us not become tired of doing good; for if we do not give up, the time will come when we will reap the harvest. So then, as often as we have the chance, we should do good to everyone, and especially to those who belong to our family in the faith.

We have seen the word 'harvest' used to represent lost souls in this world and as a picture of the end of this age. Today we see Paul using another metaphor: the harvest here stands for the good we do, the good that Jesus speaks of as riches that Christians can store up in heaven (Matthew 6:20) and that other people can recognise as God at work in them (Matthew 5:16).

Some will remember the song we used to sing back in the 1960s, 'They'll know we are Christians by our love', written by Peter Scholtes. We are often exhorted to remember that doing good to everyone is the finest form of Christian witness, but are we in danger of treading too lightly on Paul's last phrase, 'and especially to those who belong to our family in the faith' (v. 10)? Is this why we don't sing that song any longer?

Doing good has always been a paramount Christian virtue. It is one of the vital results of being filled with the Holy Spirit. We need to remind ourselves, however, that doing good is the outcome of our faith in Jesus Christ and can never be a substitute for it. Unfortunately, it is also true, as seems apparent from today's passage, that some in the Galatian church were not producing the kind of fruit that leads to eternal life. All of us are capable of 'planting' whatever we choose during each day.

Lord God, enable me to do the kind of good that will produce a harvest in the lives of others, a harvest of eternal life. Amen

PAUL GRAVELLE

You can't take it with you

'There was once a rich man who had land which bore good crops. He began to think to himself, "I don't have a place to keep all my crops… I will tear down my barns and build bigger ones, where I will store the grain… Then I will say to myself, Lucky man! You have all the good things you need for many years. Take life easy…" But God said to him, "You fool! This very night you will have to give up your life…"' And Jesus concluded, 'This is how it is with those who pile up riches for themselves but are not rich in God's sight.'

In his excellent book *Mere Christianity* (Geoffrey Bles, 1952), C.S. Lewis wrote, 'If you read history you will find that the Christians who did most for this present world were precisely those who thought most of the next.' He quotes William Wilberforce and his strenuous fight against slavery as an example and goes on to say that it is since Christians have largely ceased to think of the next world that they have become so ineffective in this one!

I am blessed to live in a retirement village. I am told that the kind of retirement villages we have here in New Zealand are a little different from those in other places, in that they are designed for active and independent retirees, rather than for those needing care. This results in such a degree of organised activity that the residents have no time to consider what comes next! Perhaps this is the intention, but it places us residents in danger of becoming like the rich man in the parable.

In his story of the rich fool, Jesus uses the harvested crops to illustrate not just our material wealth and property but the relationships, good and bad, the dealings in business, sport and leisure, and even the reputations we are able to build up. He concludes with a stern warning that none of us know how much longer we have to enjoy any of these!

Some, if not all, of the things we achieve solely for our own benefit may well have to be left in the barn.

PAUL GRAVELLE

Sowing for harvest

'Once there was a man who went out to sow grain. As he scattered the seed, some of it fell along the path, and the birds came and ate it up. Some of it fell on rocky ground, where there was little soil... But when the sun came up... the plants soon dried up. Some of the seed fell among thorn bushes, which grew up and choked the plants. But some seed fell in good soil, and the plants bore grain: some had one hundred grains, others sixty, and others thirty.'

Sowing is one of many tasks to be done before the actual harvesting of a crop can take place. Jesus uses the parable of the sower to warn his disciples that not everyone will receive his message with equal enthusiasm. He later describes the people represented by the various soil types in the parable. But nothing is said about what the harvested grain represents.

A variety of things can happen in our lives as a result of accepting the Christian message and coming to faith in Jesus Christ. Our behaviour, attitudes, relationships or whole outlook on life may change. We have already seen that the New Testament uses the idea of harvest to represent a number of different ideas, but this parable is unique in one particular way.

The parable of the sower explains how, when a seed is planted, it eventually reproduces itself many times. In John 12:24, Jesus refers to his death in this fashion: 'A grain of wheat remains no more than a single grain unless it is dropped into the ground and dies. If it does die, then it produces many grains.' Christians are the grains that are the harvest – the result – of the death of Jesus. His death has resulted in countless thousands of new grains, like you and me. He expects each of us grains to become like himself – in that we will reproduce a further harvest of grains! How are you doing in this regard?

If the message of the kingdom has found 'good soil' in our lives,
who do we see as the 100, 60 or 30 grains that we are helping
to reproduce for the coming harvest?

PAUL GRAVELLE

First fruits

But Christ has indeed been raised from the dead, the firstfruits of those who have fallen asleep. For since death came through a man, the resurrection of the dead comes also through a man. For as in Adam all die, so in Christ all will be made alive. But each in his own turn: Christ, the firstfruits; then, when he comes, those who belong to him.

In his fascinating and enlightening book *Surprised by Hope* (SPCK, 2007), Tom Wright points out that the Jewish people celebrated the beginning of harvest as well as the end. Passover was celebrated at the beginning of their wheat harvest and Pentecost similarly at the start of their barley harvest. At these festivals the firstfruits of the respective crops were presented to the Lord. They celebrated at least two harvest festivals every year.

Commenting on Paul's use of the firstfruits image in relation to Jesus' resurrection, Wright writes, 'The point of the firstfruits is that there will be many, many more.' He goes on to affirm that, just as Jesus was raised from death to live and move around here on earth, albeit in a supernaturally modified body, so will we be raised to a life here on a renewed planet earth 'when he comes again'.

Jesus is the firstfruits – the first to receive a resurrection body. But, to complete the picture, the full harvest is yet to ripen and be gathered. There are strange ideas around about what happens after death that are not to be found in scripture, but Christian creeds are unequivocal about these matters: 'We believe in one Lord, Jesus Christ'; 'He will come again in glory to judge the living and the dead, and his kingdom will have no end'; 'We look for the resurrection of the dead and the life of the world to come.'

Do we truly believe what we say, or are we still in a world of make-believe? Think again about these credal statements. Some of us recite them every Sunday. What do they really mean for you? Can you pray this prayer?

---

*Thank you, Lord, that I will meet with you
in my resurrection body in eternity. Amen*

PAUL GRAVELLE

137

Fruit of the Spirit

But the fruit of the Spirit is love, joy, peace, forbearance, kindness, goodness, faithfulness, gentleness and self-control. Against such things there is no law. Those who belong to Christ Jesus have crucified the flesh with its passions and desires. Since we live by the Spirit, let us keep in step with the Spirit.

The apostle Paul lists nine fruits of the Spirit. These are qualities that Jesus displayed and that his Spirit wants to produce in us. Similarly, in 1 Corinthians 12:8–10, Paul mentions nine gifts of the Spirit – supernatural abilities displayed by Jesus that the Spirit can also display in our lives. Both fruit and gifts are part of the harvest of good works that we were thinking about a few days ago. These two should always be seen as inseparable; the fruit of the Spirit without spiritual giftings can have only limited effect, while spiritual gifts without love and the other spiritual fruit can even be harmful.

Fruit can have two purposes. All fruits contain seed that can reproduce the parent tree, and some are also very good as food. So it is with the fruit of the Spirit. If we allow God's Spirit to help us grow more like Jesus, by developing these spiritual fruit in our lives, we may find that people will notice and ask what has caused the change. But even if they do not, it is more than likely that, as the fruit of the Spirit ripens in our lives, we will find we are becoming more of a blessing to others anyway.

We probably recognise that some of these qualities are natural to our personalities, and that there are some people who display this fruit without demonstrating any of the behaviours we normally regard as Christian, such as attending church. Let us rejoice and be glad wherever we see this happening and always pray for more of it. At the same time, we need to recognise that the reverse applies; we can sometimes produce the opposite sort of fruit ourselves. We all need to confess to producing bad fruit from time to time. God's forgiveness will see it fall away!

What fresh fruit of the Spirit might God want to develop in your life?

PAUL GRAVELLE

The ultimate harvest

Then another angel came... and cried out in a loud voice... 'Use your sickle and reap the harvest, because the time has come; the earth is ripe for the harvest!' Then the one who sat on the cloud swung his sickle on the earth, and the earth's harvest was reaped... Then another angel... shouted in a loud voice... 'Use your sickle, and cut the grapes from the vineyard of the earth, because the grapes are ripe!' So the angel... cut the grapes from the vine, and threw them into the wine press of God's furious anger.

Why is it that we can be so resistant to the idea of God's judgement? We happily condemn human evil wherever we see it, but we seem unable to accord God the same privilege! We have seen that in his interpretation of the parable of the weeds, Jesus was pretty blunt about the place of judgement at the end of this age, but we are usually reluctant to talk about it.

John's vision is one of many that are set out in his Revelation. They were recorded to encourage Christians who were suffering severe persecution, giving them assurance that their sufferings were not in vain, that God was in charge of their eternal future and that God would finally vindicate them in the face of their oppressors.

Lurid though the vision is, the future it portrays is clear enough in its implications. John's vision speaks of two kinds of harvest: one that is fit for God's kingdom and another that he will reject as unfit. As Christians, we cannot close our eyes to the inevitability of God's judgement and to the fact that the final harvest will certainly involve a divine dealing with all that is evil.

Our call as church is to proclaim the good news that Jesus 'will come again in glory to judge' and to establish his kingdom on planet earth. Have you noticed that, in the prayer that Jesus taught his disciples, the first petition that we are encouraged to make is about this?

Our Father in heaven, hallowed be your name. Your Kingdom come, your will be done on earth, as it is in heaven. Amen

PAUL GRAVELLE

This page is left blank for your notes

Reading *New Daylight* in a group

SALLY WELCH

I am aware that although some of you cherish the moments of quiet during the day which enable you to read and reflect on the passages we offer you in *New Daylight*, other readers prefer to study in small groups, to enable conversation and discussion and the sharing of insights. With this in mind, here are some ideas for discussion starters within a study group. Some of the questions are generic and can be applied to any set of contributions within this issue; others are specific to certain sets of readings. I hope they generate some interesting reflections and conversations!

General discussion starters

These can be used for any study series within this issue. Remember there are no right or wrong answers – these questions are simply to enable a group to engage in conversation.

- What do you think is the main idea or theme of the author in this series? Do you think they succeeded in communicating this to you, or were you more interested in the side issues?

- Have you had any experience of the issues that are raised in the study? How have they affected your life?

- What evidence does the author use to support their ideas? Do they use personal observations and experience, facts, quotations from other authorities? Which appeals to you most?

- Does the author make a 'call to action'? Is that call realistic and achievable? Do you think their ideas will work in the secular world?

- Can you identify specific passages that struck you personally – as interesting, profound, difficult to understand or illuminating?

- Did you learn something new reading this series? Will you think differently about some things, and if so, what are they?

Questions for specific series
My favourite prayers (Lakshmi Jeffreys)
Lakshmi uses a wide variety of prayers as part of deepening her relationship with God. Which are your favourite prayers? What would be your 'desert island' prayer? Does the way you pray illustrate the way you think about God? Do you think this is a true representation of him?

Resilience (Tony Horsfall)
Do you agree with Tony's definition of 'spiritual resilience'? How resilient do you think you are? In what circumstances do you have most need of resilience – in the issues of daily life or in times of major crisis? How far do the examples from the Bible resonate with your own experience?

The presence of God (John Ryeland)
What does the presence of God mean to you? Are there occasions in your life when you have felt the presence of God particularly strongly? Are there times of doubt and difficulty when you have been afraid that God is absent? How have you reacted to these times?

During the season of harvest, we reflect on how much we have received from God and give thanks for all his blessings. We also look again at our own giving – not just money, but also our time and talents – and ask ourselves whether we are doing our part in helping to gather in God's harvest.

Author profile: Tony Horsfall

Can you briefly describe your spiritual journey – when did you first become a Christian and where has this taken you?

I was converted when I was 14 in the Methodist chapel in the Yorkshire mining village where I grew up. Almost immediately I had a sense that God wanted me to serve him. After leaving school I took a degree in theology at the London Bible College, where I met Evelyn, who became my wife. We served in Borneo with the Overseas Missionary Fellowship for eight years. After our return I was pastor of a local church, then headed up a missions training programme before launching out on my own ministry, Charis Training, in 2002. I love to lead retreats, to speak at conferences for mission partners and to write. I'm also very involved in my local church.

You have written several books – which one is your favourite?

Each one has a special place in my heart, but probably *Rhythms of Grace*, since it was the first and has impacted so many people.

You write about resilience in this issue. How did you become interested in this subject?

I love sport, and resilience is a key characteristic of those who are successful, often against the odds. I have a particular care for those in full-time ministry, and again it seems that if they are to thrive they will need resilience. But I know from my own life how important it is to persevere, especially in the hard times. If we can increase our ability to endure, then so much the better.

Which spiritual writers have influenced you and in what ways?

I love to read anything by John Stott; his Bible teaching is superb. Henri Nouwen and Andrew Murray helped me to understand the inner life and being loved by God. Joyce Huggett introduced me to contemplative spirituality, so her writing has been influential. Eugene Peterson gives a contemporary perspective on Christian ministry that I like. But I enjoy reading widely and try to keep abreast of current thinking.

Where would you like to be in ten years?

Still alive! I'll be 79 then, so if I am still active and serving the Lord I will be well satisfied.

Recommended reading

Books on prayer can so often make us feel challenged but guilty. Not this one! *Prayer in the Making* is a book for everyone wanting to pray more confidently. Because we are all different, we need to find the prayer life that fits with who God made us to be. Lyndall Bywater explores twelve different types of prayer, helping us to find the ones which best suit us and our lifestyles. She certainly challenges us, but leaves us ready to talk confidently with God.

The following is taken from Chapter One, 'Encounter'.

If you were an ancient Roman, prayer was a complicated business. Firstly, you had to have a shrine somewhere in your home, preferably with a fire that burned 24 hours a day, and that's where you'd keep the statues of your favourite gods. You'd be expected to make time to pray at your shrine at least once a day, but it wasn't a straightforward business. You'd have to make sure you were clean and tidy, because dirt and unsavoury smells counted as bad omens, and they could cancel out any praying you did. You'd have to prepare your offering, to convince the gods of your sincerity, and then you'd have to make sure you knew exactly what you were going to pray.

In fact, if you didn't have a friendly priest on hand to lead you through some top-of-the-range prayers, you'd probably choose to write a prayer out, to make sure it said exactly what you wanted it to say. The Roman gods were famous for being picky when it came to prayers; they would take offence if you got their names wrong, or if you asked them for too much without flattering them enough first. They were highly legalistic, so Roman prayers read more like legal contracts, because the gods would use any loophole they could to get out of answering your requests. And if all of that wasn't complicated enough, you had to be able to say your prayers without slipping up once. If you got a single word wrong, then you'd have to make a *piaculum* – a little sacrifice to apologise for messing up – and then you'd have to start the whole session over again.

Jesus, God made man, stepped right into the middle of that Roman empire, with all its convoluted religion, and spoke these few ground-breaking sentences:

But when you pray, go into your room, close the door and pray to your Father, who is unseen. Then your Father, who sees what is done in secret, will reward you. And when you pray, do not keep on babbling like pagans, for they think they will be heard because of their many words. Do not be like them, for your Father knows what you need before you ask him (Matthew 6:6–8).

Most of his listeners would have been Jews, but they would have known about Roman prayer, and these words would have had a special resonance for them as they watched Roman culture seeping ever further into their lives. Jesus was turning everything on its head. In the empire of Rome, prayer was a matter of scrupulous preparation, trying to get it right with your lengthy, perfectly formed compositions, and still having no guarantee whatsoever that you'd been heard. In the kingdom of God, prayer would be a simple matter of stepping aside from life to be in the company of the Father, expressing yourself in uncomplicated sincerity, and knowing beyond all doubt that you'd been heard. Prayer wasn't to be difficult, complicated and inaccessible; it was to be as simple as sitting down to talk with a loved one.

John's vision on Patmos reminds us that we come to one who is holy, exalted and glorious, and we should never lose sight of that, but Jesus' words here in the sermon on the mount remind us that our great and mighty God doesn't want us to put up a front to impress him. He knows and loves us just as we are, and he means prayer to start in the most unpretentious corners of our hearts.

Trying to impress the divine wasn't just a Roman trait. Jesus' own people had their fair share of religious nonsense. During one of his other teaching sessions, he told the story of two men who prayed (Luke 18:9–14). The first was a religious man who knew all the right forms and rituals, and who was pretty convinced of his own prowess when it came to prayer. The other man was a tax collector – which, in Jesus' time, was code for 'nasty bloke' – and he prayed a rather clumsy, broken prayer from the depths of his soul. The religious man's prayer was all about proving himself to God. The tax collector's prayer was all about bringing his flaws and failings to God and asking for mercy.

There is no such thing as being too bad for God. No matter who you are, what you're like or what you've done, that 'inner room' of prayer is open to you. It's not a literal inner room (though it is a good idea to find a quiet place when you want to have an honest, in-depth conversation with God); it is the inner room of yourself – the place where the real you lives, where all the pretences are stripped away and where you hide the tenderest parts of yourself. That is the place where the one who loves you wants to meet with you in prayer.

In Luke's gospel, this story is followed by another one with the same message. There were parents who wanted their children to see Jesus, but the disciples decided that wasn't an important enough use of his time, so they sent them away (Luke 18:15–17). It is one of the few times when we see Jesus angry. He was incensed at the idea that these little ones were somehow less welcome or less worthy of his time than anyone else. These were the very ones he felt at home with, because these were the ones who reminded him of home.

Christian prayer means starting small. If you ever feel you're not sophisticated enough, theological enough, articulate enough or holy enough to pray, then you are in exactly the right frame of mind for an encounter with God. He loves simplicity, honesty and humility; those are the hallmarks of his kingdom, and when he finds them in you, he feels completely at home.

To order a copy of this book, please use the order form on page 149.

Tony Horsfall and Debbie Hawker encourage us to develop our resilience and to prepare ourselves for the challenges that life throws at us in an increasingly difficult world. Through biblical wisdom and psychological insight, they show us how to understand ourselves better, appreciate our areas of strength and strengthen our areas of weakness. Read this book if you want a faith that persists to the finishing line.

Resilience in Life and Faith
Finding your strength in God
Tony Horsfall and Debbie Hawker
978 0 85746 734 8 £9.99
brfonline.org.uk

To order

Online: **brfonline.org.uk**
Telephone: +44 (0)1865 319700
Mon–Fri 9.15–17.30

Delivery times within the UK are normally 15 working days. Prices are correct at the time of going to press but may change without prior notice.

Title	Price	Qty	Total
Prayer in the Making	£8.99		
Resilience in Life and Faith	£9.99		

POSTAGE AND PACKING CHARGES			
Order value	UK	Europe	Rest of world
Under £7.00	£2.00	£5.00	£7.00
£7.00–£29.99	£3.00	£9.00	£15.00
£30.00 and over	FREE	£9.00 + 15% of order value	£15.00 + 20% of order value

Total value of books	
Postage and packing	
Total for this order	

Please complete in BLOCK CAPITALS

Title _____ First name/initials _____ Surname _____

Address _____

_____ Postcode _____

Acc. No. _____ Telephone _____

Email _____

Method of payment

❑ Cheque (made payable to BRF) ❑ MasterCard / Visa

Card no. ☐☐☐☐ ☐☐☐☐ ☐☐☐☐ ☐☐☐☐

Expires end ☐☐ ☐☐ Security code* ☐☐☐ Last 3 digits on the reverse of the card

Signature* _____ Date _____ / _____ / _____
*ESSENTIAL IN ORDER TO PROCESS YOUR ORDER

Please return this form to:
BRF, 15 The Chambers, Vineyard, Abingdon OX14 3FE | **enquiries@brf.org.uk**
To read our terms and find out about cancelling your order, please visit **brfonline.org.uk/terms**.

The Bible Reading Fellowship (BRF) is a Registered Charity (233280)

How to encourage Bible reading in your church

BRF has been helping individuals connect with the Bible for over 90 years. We want to support churches as they seek to encourage church members into regular Bible reading.

Order a Bible reading resources pack

This pack is designed to give your church the tools to publicise our Bible reading notes. It includes:

- Sample Bible reading notes for your congregation to try.
- Publicity resources, including a poster.
- A church magazine feature about Bible reading notes.

The pack is free, but we welcome a £5 donation to cover the cost of postage. If you require a pack to be sent outside the UK or require a specific number of sample Bible reading notes, please contact us for postage costs. More information about what the current pack contains is available on our website.

How to order and find out more

- Visit **biblereadingnotes.org.uk/for-churches**
- Telephone BRF on +44 (0)1865 319700 Mon–Fri 9.15–17.30
- Write to us at BRF, 15 The Chambers, Vineyard, Abingdon OX14 3FE

Keep informed about our latest initiatives

We are continuing to develop resources to help churches encourage people into regular Bible reading, wherever they are on their journey. Join our email list at **brfonline.org.uk/signup** to stay informed about the latest initiatives that your church could benefit from.

Transforming lives and communities

BRF is a charity that is passionate about making a difference through the Christian faith. We want to see lives and communities transformed through our creative programmes and resources for individuals, churches and schools. We are doing this by resourcing:

- **Christian growth and understanding of the Bible.** Through our Bible reading notes, books, digital resources, conferences and other events, we're resourcing individuals, groups and leaders in churches for their own spiritual journey and for their ministry.
- **Church outreach in the local community.** BRF is the home of Messy Church and The Gift of Years, programmes that churches are embracing to great effect as they seek to engage with their communities.
- **Teaching Christianity in primary schools.** Our Barnabas in Schools team is working with primary-aged children and their teachers, enabling them to explore Christianity creatively and confidently within the school curriculum.
- **Children's and family ministry.** Through our Parenting for Faith programme, websites and published resources, we're working with churches and families, enabling children and adults alike to explore Christianity creatively and bring the Bible alive.

Do you share our vision?

Sales of our books and Bible reading notes cover the cost of producing them. However, our other programmes are funded primarily by donations, grants and legacies. If you share our vision, would you help us to transform even more lives and communities? Your prayers and financial support are vital for the work that we do. You could:

- support BRF's ministry with a regular donation (at **brf.org.uk/donate**);
- support us with a one-off gift (use the form on pages 153–54);
- consider leaving a gift to BRF in your will (see page 152);
- encourage your church to support BRF as part of your church's giving to home mission – perhaps focusing on a specific area of our ministry, or a particular member of our Barnabas in Schools team.
- most important of all, support BRF with your prayers.

Spiritual care from the cradle to the grave

In 1942, as war raged across Europe and in the Pacific, William Beveridge published a radical report. In it, he argued for a state-run social security system that would fight the 'five giants' – want, disease, squalor, ignorance and idleness.

When World War II ended in 1945, the launch of the welfare state was announced, and Beveridge's vision became a reality. Among other things, free education, social housing and a national health service (the NHS) providing care 'from the cradle to the grave' would soon be available to all.

The NHS has revolutionised Britain and its commitment to providing lifelong care means that many of us are living longer, healthier lives. Physical and emotional care are an important part of the picture, but they're not the only necessities for true well-being. Research has shown that attending to spiritual needs is just as important for our overall health.

At The Bible Reading Fellowship (BRF), we are passionate about helping people of all ages explore Christianity and grow in faith. Just like Beveridge, we want to provide care from the cradle to the grave. Whether you're a child of five attending Messy Church for the very first time or nearly 95 and enjoying the visits of an Anna Chaplain through BRF's The Gift of Years programme, we believe we have something that will help you take those important next steps on your spiritual journey.

If you share our vision for transforming lives of all ages through the Christian faith, would you consider leaving a gift in your will to BRF? We value every gift, small or large, and use them for significant projects with lasting impact..

For further information about making a gift to BRF in your will, please visit **brf.org.uk/lastingdifference**, contact Sophie Aldred on **+44 (0)1865 319700** or email **giving@brf.org.uk**.

Whatever you can do or give, we thank you for your support.

I would like to make a gift to support BRF. Please use my gift for:

☐ where it is needed most ☐ Barnabas in Schools ☐ Parenting for Faith

☐ Messy Church ☐ The Gift of Years

Title	First name/initials	Surname

Address

Postcode

Email

Telephone

Signature	Date

giftaid it You can add an extra 25p to every £1 you give.

Please treat as Gift Aid donations all qualifying gifts of money made

☐ today, ☐ in the past four years, ☐ and in the future.

I am a UK taxpayer and understand that if I pay less Income Tax and/or Capital Gains Tax in the current tax year than the amount of Gift Aid claimed on all my donations, it is my responsibility to pay any difference.

☐ My donation does not qualify for Gift Aid.

Please notify BRF if you want to cancel this Gift Aid declaration, change your name or home address, or no longer pay sufficient tax on your income and/or capital gains.

Please complete other side of form ➜

Please return this form to:
BRF, 15 The Chambers, Vineyard, Abingdon OX14 3FE

BRF

The Bible Reading Fellowship is a Registered Charity (233280)

Regular giving

By Direct Debit: You can set up a Direct Debit quickly and easily at **brf.org.uk/donate**

By Standing Order: Please contact our Fundraising Administrator +44 (0)1235 462305 | **giving@brf.org.uk**

One-off donation

Please accept my gift of:

☐ £10   ☐ £50   ☐ £100   Other £ ☐☐☐☐☐☐

by (*delete as appropriate*):

☐ Cheque/Charity Voucher payable to 'BRF'

☐ MasterCard/Visa/Debit card/Charity card

Name on card

Card no.

Expires end [M M] [Y Y]   Security code* ☐☐☐

*Last 3 digits on the reverse of the card
ESSENTIAL IN ORDER TO PROCESS YOUR PAYMENT

Signature

Date

☐ I would like to leave a gift in my will to BRF.

For more information, visit **brf.org.uk/lastingdifference**

For help or advice regarding making a gift, please contact our Fundraising Administrator +44 (0)1235 462305

↰ Please complete other side of form

Please return this form to:

BRF, 15 The Chambers, Vineyard, Abingdon OX14 3FE

❦ **BRF**

The Bible Reading Fellowship is a Registered Charity (233280)

ND0119

NEW DAYLIGHT GIFT SUBSCRIPTION FORM

☐ I would like to give a gift subscription (please provide both names and addresses):

Title _____ First name/initials _____ Surname _____

Address _____

_____ Postcode _____

Telephone _____ Email _____

Gift subscription name _____

Gift subscription address _____

_____ Postcode _____

Gift message (20 words max. or include your own gift card):

_____

_____

Please send *New Daylight* beginning with the September 2019 / January 2020 / May 2020 issue (*delete as appropriate*):

(*please tick box*)	UK	Europe	Rest of world
New Daylight 1-year subscription	☐ £17.40	☐ £25.50	☐ £29.40
New Daylight 3-year subscription	☐ £49.50	N/A	N/A
New Daylight Deluxe	☐ £21.90	☐ £32.40	☐ £38.40

Total enclosed £ _____ (cheques should be made payable to 'BRF')

Please charge my MasterCard / Visa ☐ Debit card ☐ with £ _____

Card no. ☐☐☐☐ ☐☐☐☐ ☐☐☐☐ ☐☐☐☐

Expires end ☐☐ ☐☐ Security code* ☐☐☐ Last 3 digits on the reverse of the card

Signature* _____ Date _____ / _____ / _____

*ESSENTIAL IN ORDER TO PROCESS YOUR PAYMENT

To set up a Direct Debit, please also complete the Direct Debit instruction on page 159 and return it to BRF with this form.

Please return this form with the appropriate payment to:
BRF, 15 The Chambers, Vineyard, Abingdon OX14 3FE

BRF

To read our terms and find out about cancelling your order, please visit **brfonline.org.uk/terms**.

The Bible Reading Fellowship is a Registered Charity (233280)

You can pay for your annual subscription to our Bible reading notes using Direct Debit. You need only give your bank details once, and the payment is made automatically every year until you cancel it. If you would like to pay by Direct Debit, please use the form opposite, entering your BRF account number under 'Reference number'.

You are fully covered by the Direct Debit Guarantee:

The Direct Debit Guarantee

- This Guarantee is offered by all banks and building societies that accept instructions to pay Direct Debits.

- If there are any changes to the amount, date or frequency of your Direct Debit, The Bible Reading Fellowship will notify you 10 working days in advance of your account being debited or as otherwise agreed. If you request The Bible Reading Fellowship to collect a payment, confirmation of the amount and date will be given to you at the time of the request.

- If an error is made in the payment of your Direct Debit, by The Bible Reading Fellowship or your bank or building society, you are entitled to a full and immediate refund of the amount paid from your bank or building society.

- If you receive a refund you are not entitled to, you must pay it back when The Bible Reading Fellowship asks you to.

- You can cancel a Direct Debit at any time by simply contacting your bank or building society. Written confirmation may be required. Please also notify us.

The Bible Reading Fellowship

Instruction to your bank or building society to pay by Direct Debit

Please fill in the whole form using a ballpoint pen and return it to:
BRF, 15 The Chambers, Vineyard, Abingdon OX14 3FE

Service User Number: | 5 | 5 | 8 | 2 | 2 | 9 |

Name and full postal address of your bank or building society

To: The Manager	Bank/Building Society
Address	
	Postcode

Name(s) of account holder(s)

Branch sort code

Bank/Building Society account number

Reference number

Instruction to your Bank/Building Society
Please pay The Bible Reading Fellowship Direct Debits from the account detailed in this instruction, subject to the safeguards assured by the Direct Debit Guarantee. I understand that this instruction may remain with The Bible Reading Fellowship and, if so, details will be passed electronically to my bank/building society.

Signature(s)

Banks and Building Societies may not accept Direct Debit instructions for some types of account.

BRF

Transforming
lives and communities

Christian growth and understanding of the Bible

Resourcing individuals, groups and leaders in churches for their own spiritual journey and for their ministry

Church outreach in the local community

Offering two programmes that churches are embracing to great effect as they seek to engage with their local communities and transform lives

Teaching Christianity in primary schools

Working with children and teachers to explore Christianity creatively and confidently

Children's and family ministry

Working with churches and families to explore Christianity creatively and bring the Bible alive

parenting for faith

Visit **brf.org.uk** for more information on BRF's work

brf.org.uk

The Bible Reading Fellowship (BRF) is a Registered Charity (No. 233280)